LET'S STUDY
1 TIMOTHY

Series Editor: SINCLAIR B. FERGUSON

Let's Study

1 TIMOTHY

W. John Cook

THE BANNER OF TRUTH TRUST

THE BANNER OF TRUTH TRUST
3 Murrayfield Road, Edinburgh EH12 6EL, UK
P.O. Box 621, Carlisle, PA 17013, USA

*

© W. John Cook 2009
ISBN: 978 1 84871 047 4

*

Typeset in 11 / 12.5 pt Ehrhardt MT at the
Banner of Truth Trust, Edinburgh

Printed in the U.S.A. by
Versa Press, Inc.,
East Peoria, IL

Contents

[v]

Publisher's Preface

*L*et's *Study 1 Timothy* is part of a series of books which explain and apply the message of Scripture. The series is designed to meet a specific and important need in the church. While not technical commentaries, the volumes comment on the text of a biblical book; and, without being merely lists of practical applications, they are concerned with the ways in which the teaching of Scripture can affect and transform our lives today. Understanding the Bible's message and applying its teaching are the aims.

Like other volumes in the series, *Let's Study 1 Timothy* seeks to combine explanation and application. Its concern is to be helpful to ordinary Christian people by encouraging them to understand the message of the Bible and apply it to their own lives. The reader in view is not the person who is interested in all the detailed questions which fascinate the scholar, although behind the writing of each study lies an appreciation for careful and detailed scholarship. The aim is exposition of Scripture written in the language of a friend, seated alongside you with an open Bible.

Let's Study 1 Timothy is designed to be used in various contexts. It can be used simply as an aid for individual Bible study. Some may find it helpful to use in their devotions with husband or wife, or to read in the context of the whole family.

In order to make these studies more useful, not only for individual use but also for group study in Sunday School classes and home, church, or college, study guide material will be found on p. 119. Sometimes we come away frustrated rather than helped by group discussions. Frequently that is because we have been encouraged to discuss a passage of Scripture which we do not understand very well in the first place. Understanding must always be the foundation for enriching discussion and for thoughtful, practical application. Thus, following the exposition of 1 Timothy, the additional material provides questions to encourage personal thought and study, or to be used as discussion starters. The Group Study Guide divides the material into thirteen sections and provides direction for leading and participating in group study and discussion.

Author's Preface

The series of which *Let's Study 1 Timothy* is a part is designed to help Christians understand the revelation of truth that God has given to us in the holy Scriptures. When we become Christians we are enrolled in Christ's school of discipleship and he is concerned that by the application of our minds to God's Word we should know him better and respond to his guidance in the way we live. It is the basic and important means by which we can obey the command of 2 Peter 3:18, 'Grow in the grace and knowledge of our Lord and Saviour Jesus Christ.'

The Lord had commissioned his apostles to make disciples (*Matt.* 28:19), and the result of Paul's gospel preaching at Derbe was that many disciples were made (*Acts* 14:21). A disciple is a learner or student of a teacher, and Jesus said to those who came to him for rest, 'Learn from me' (*Matt.* 11:28–29). The term 'disciples' was widely used of believers in the Lord Jesus Christ before they were called 'Christians' in Antioch (*Acts* 11:26).

The aim of this commentary is to help its readers to make progress as disciples by means of careful explanation of the contents of this epistle and by relevant application to their daily lives. We may be encouraged in our study to know that all God's children are taught by God (*Isa.* 54:13, *John* 6:45), and he has given us the Holy Spirit to lead us into all truth. No one should be hindered from reading because they don't feel they are clever enough to understand and benefit, for God is the best of teachers! Of course, we must seek his help in prayer: 'Teach me your statutes' (*Psa.* 119:26), and, 'Teach me to do your will, for you are my God!' (*Psa.* 143:10).

Acknowledgement

This commentary is submitted with thanks to God for all the benefit gained through Banner of Truth publications and ministers' conferences over forty-five years, and for the personal encouragement given by the Rev. Iain H. Murray.

Introduction

The two epistles to Timothy and the epistle to Titus are regularly linked together under the title, the 'Pastoral Epistles', because they are addressed to two men who were to act as the apostle's assistants in shepherding the growing Christian church according to the divine pattern. These epistles were written especially to provide God's rules for the organization of the church and its many congregations, in order that sound doctrine would be communicated and preserved, with the aid of right government.

Each of these epistles claims very clearly to have been written by the apostle Paul and, despite much 'scholarly' denial over the last two hundred years, our conviction about the sanctity of truth leads us gladly to receive them as part of the infallible Word of God. In doing so we find ourselves in the good company of many of the early Christian writers, for there is documentary evidence from the early part of the second century that they were accepted as written by Paul with divine authority. A century ago J. H. Bernard claimed, 'There is a continuous testimony to the circulation of the Pastoral epistles in the East as far back as the year 116 AD', that is, probably less than fifty years after the apostle's death. More recently William Hendriksen and many other evangelical scholars have confidently asserted that within the Christian church there was a strong and uniform tradition ascribing the Pastorals to the apostle Paul (see Hendriksen, *New Testament Commentary: 1 & 2 Timothy and Titus*, Banner of Truth, 1960, pp. 4–33).

These epistles were almost certainly written after Paul had been released from his imprisonment at Rome, where for two years he lived in his own hired house, 'proclaiming the kingdom of God and teaching about the Lord Jesus Christ with all boldness and without hindrance' (*Acts* 28:16, 30–31). We presume that, as indicated in Philippians 2:19, 23, Paul sent Timothy to Philippi and then, it seems, on to Ephesus, or accompanied him there, where he urged him to remain to accomplish his mission. Paul had meanwhile gone into Macedonia (*1 Tim.* 1:3), and particularly to Philippi, keeping his promise in Philippians 2:24. From there he wrote 1 Timothy and Titus, but 2 Timothy belongs to a later period, when Paul was again in Rome. He expected then to conclude his ministry there, as his words reveal, 'The time of my departure has come. I have fought the good fight, I have finished the race' (*2 Tim.* 4:6–7).

The view that Paul wrote the Pastoral Epistles subsequent to the history recorded in the Acts of the Apostles accords with the statement of Eusebius in his *Church History* that Paul was twice imprisoned at Rome. The contents of these letters are most obviously related to, and necessary for, the time when the apostles were no longer present to instruct the Christian church in person, and they are an important element in God's provision for subsequent centuries.

In the *Institutes of the Christian Religion,* Book IV, ch. 8, sect. 9, John Calvin emphasized the difference between the apostles and their successors in the Christian ministry: 'They were sure and authentic amanuenses [scribes or secretaries] of the Holy Spirit; and, therefore, their writings are to be regarded as the oracles of God, whereas others have no other office than to teach what is delivered and sealed in the holy Scriptures.'

It is important today to recognize in our Bible studies that God himself is our only Master in the realm of spiritual truth and that no one is warranted to introduce other teaching into the church. Martin Luther encouraged us in a hymn to ask the aid of the Holy Spirit:

> *From every error keep us free,*
> *Let none but Christ our master be,*
> *That we in living faith abide,*
> *In Him with all our might confide.*

Translated by Catherine Winkworth

Outline of 1 Timothy

CHAPTER 1

The address and greetings of the epistle (1–2)
Timothy's task at Ephesus (3–7)
The proper use of God's law (8–11)
Paul's thanksgiving to God for his abundant grace (12–17)
Paul's solemn charge to Timothy (18–20)

CHAPTER 2

Public prayer in the worshipping congregation (1–7)
Directions for congregational worship (8–10)
Teaching about the life of women in the church (11–15)

CHAPTER 3

Qualifications for church elders (1-7).
Requirements for deacons (8–13)
The church of the living God (14–16)

I

Address and Greetings

Paul, an apostle of Christ Jesus, by command of God our Saviour and of Christ Jesus our hope, ² to Timothy, my true child in the faith: Grace, mercy, and peace from God the Father and Christ Jesus our Lord (1 Tim. 1:1–2).

The form of this letter, in which the author begins with his name, reflects the normal practice at the time, as illustrated in Acts 23:26 where Luke includes a letter from a Roman officer. It begins, 'Claudius Lysias, to his Excellency the governor Felix, greetings.' So here Paul identifies himself as the author, addresses the letter to Timothy, and then adds a distinctively Christian greeting. Each of these elements is worthy of comment.

Paul emphasizes at the beginning that he is writing as an apostle of Jesus Christ by divine command and not simply as an older and more experienced Christian worker whom Timothy would greatly respect. He is not simply passing on good advice drawn from his long ministry as a preacher and evangelist but communicating the message which God had entrusted to him.

It is important therefore that we consider its significance, as a reminder that the Lord Jesus Christ had directly invested the apostles with his own authority to teach and command Christians and churches what they should believe and how they should behave. This letter then must be received like the messages given by God's servants the prophets of the Old Testament as his Word, so that it could equally be prefaced by the charge, 'Hear the word of the Lord.' It bore then, and continually possesses, the same authority as the words of Jesus that have been recorded for us in the four

Gospels of the New Testament. God had chosen this method of instructing believers in the context of their different circumstances, so that there was an immediate discernible relevance to them, and when the New Testament was complete the Christian church was fully provided with all necessary teaching for its growth and government. Jonathan Edwards commented helpfully on this fact:

> There was now completed an established written revelation of the mind and will of God, wherein God has fully recorded a standing and all-sufficient rule for his church in all ages (*Charity and Its Fruits*, 1852, repr. Banner of Truth, 1969, p. 312)

Though we are familiar with the name Jesus Christ (sometimes given in reverse order, *Christ Jesus*), even perhaps *because* we are well acquainted with it, there is great benefit to be gained by recognizing that in itself it reveals significant truth about who he is. The name *Jesus* is the Greek equivalent of the Hebrew *Joshua*, and directly indicates that he was a real human being, from his conception in Mary's womb, which itself was due to a unique, miraculous working of the Holy Spirit. His mother was informed by the angel Gabriel that this would take place, and she was commanded to give the name Jesus to her son, who was also the Son of God (*Luke* 1:31,35). In Matthew 1:21–22 an angel of the Lord appeared to Joseph, who was betrothed to Mary, and explained how Mary had conceived, so that he should not be afraid to take her as his wife. The angel also renewed the command, 'You shall call his name Jesus', and added the reason, 'for he will save his people from their sins.'

Christ is really a title, 'Anointed One', exactly equivalent to the Old Testament term *Messiah*. This was particularly used of the promised Saviour whose coming and ministry were predicted in many prophecies. When Jesus spoke in the synagogue at Nazareth, where he had been brought up, he read from Isaiah 61:1, 'The Spirit of the Lord GOD is upon me, because the LORD has anointed me', and then announced, 'Today this Scripture has been fulfilled in your hearing' (*Luke* 4:21). This truth that his hearers then dismissed in unbelief was confessed by the apostle Peter in Matthew 16:16, 'You are the Christ, the Son of the living God', and later proclaimed in his sermon at Pentecost (*Acts* 2:30–31 and 36), and explained at Caesarea in Acts 10:38, 'God anointed Jesus of Nazareth with the Holy Spirit.'

The fact that Jesus of Nazareth was the Christ was part of Paul's earliest preaching (*Acts* 9:22) and clearly was foundational to his whole life and ministry. Its significance is well described in the *Westminster Larger Catechism*, Answer 42:

> Our Mediator was called Christ, because he was anointed with the Holy Ghost above measure; and so set apart, and fully furnished with all authority and ability, to execute the offices of prophet, priest and king of his church . . .

We note also that he is called *our Lord* in verse 2, a title that not merely indicates that he is our Master but also identifies him as true and eternal God, for the Greek term *Kurios* was used of the LORD in the familiar Greek translation of the Hebrew Bible, the Septuagint (LXX). This truth is also evident from the conjunction of God and Christ Jesus as the joint source of the commandment that Paul obeyed and the greeting he conveyed.

Christ Jesus is also described here as *our hope*. The Psalmist affirms the same thing: 'For you, O Lord, are my hope' (*Psa.* 71:5), and Psalm 146:5 teaches, 'Blessed is he . . . whose hope is in the LORD his God.' He is the foundation, the author and the embodiment of our hope, for he has secured for us our eternal inheritance, and Christ in us is the believer's 'hope of glory' (*Col.* 1:27).

The phrase, *God our Saviour,* found twice more in this letter (2:3, 4:10), and three times in Titus (1:3, 2:10, and 3:4), deserves a little attention, as it is the first time that Paul calls God the Father 'Saviour'. The work of man's salvation from sin is of course frequently ascribed to God the Father, as in Titus 3:5–7, 'He saved us . . . according to his own mercy, by the washing of regeneration and renewal of the Holy Spirit, whom he poured out on us richly through Jesus Christ our Saviour.' In this work of salvation the Lord Jesus is the Mediator (2:5), for it was he who bore our sins in his own body on the tree (*1 Pet.* 2:24), so that we quite naturally and properly tend to refer to him as our Saviour. We need to realize however that the term Saviour has a wider scope of reference than saving from sin, for it conveys the sense of Benefactor, as the Psalmist wrote of God, 'You are good and do good' (*Psa.*

119:68). As Paul taught the pagans at Lystra, the living God whom he served 'did good by giving you rains from heaven and fruitful seasons, satisfying your hearts with food and gladness' (*Acts* 14:17). This meaning becomes obvious in 1 Timothy 4:10 where Paul refers to the living God 'who is the Saviour of all people, especially of those who believe'.

We know quite a lot about Paul, formerly known as Saul of Tarsus, and it is profitable also to learn a little about Timothy to whom the letter is addressed. The description given him here, *my true child in the faith*, itself encourages us to gather from other scriptures further biographical details about him. Timothy is first mentioned in Acts 16:1–2 as a resident of Lystra. He had probably been brought to faith through the preaching ministry of Paul on the occasion recorded in Acts 14. Later, with the commendation of his fellow Christians, he was ordained to the Christian ministry (*1 Tim.* 4:14, *2 Tim.* 1:6). Though his father was Greek, he had been blessed with a believing Jewish mother, Eunice, and grandmother, Lois (*2 Tim.* 1:5), so that from childhood he had known the holy Scriptures, or sacred writings, which are able to make one wise for salvation through faith in Christ Jesus (*2 Tim.* 1:5; 3:15).

Timothy had benefited from the privilege of accompanying Paul on his second missionary journey (*Acts* 16:1-4), and during this time he was also employed on various tasks to establish infant churches in the faith (*Acts* 17:14; 20:22, *1 Thess.* 3:2). In 1 Corinthians 4:17 the apostle described him as 'my beloved and faithful child in the Lord', who was sent to remind them of his ways in Christ, as he taught everywhere in every church. He also commended him later in Philippians 2:22: 'As a son with a father he has served with me in the gospel.' There was obviously a close bond of Christian fellowship between these two men. This is evident in 2 Timothy, for in 1:3–4, Paul writes, 'I remember you constantly in my prayers night and day . . . I long to see you that I may be filled with joy', and in 4:9, 21, 'Do your best to come to me soon', and, 'Do your best to come before winter.'

The greeting of this letter has an extra ingredient, *mercy*, added to the more familiar elements, *grace* and *peace*, found in all of Paul's other letters from Romans to Philemon. Lest our familiarity should

[4]

hinder our appreciation of these important nouns, we ought to remind ourselves that the essential nature of *grace* is that it is God's own unmerited favour and well expresses the absolute freeness of his love to men in salvation: 'By grace you have been saved' (*Eph.* 2:5,8). Later in this chapter Paul declared that for him, 'the grace of our Lord overflowed' (verse 14), and this should stimulate the realization in every Christian of our total indebtedness to God's grace. Each believer should acknowledge with the apostle that it is 'by the grace of God I am what I am' (*1 Cor.* 15:10), and rejoice that the whole outworking of God's eternal plan of salvation is to the praise of his glorious grace (*Eph.* 1:6).

Divine *mercy* is exercised towards men, as considered in their pitiable condition of misery due to the consequences of sin, in order to release them from their wretched state. There is included in it the tenderness of divine compassion, and both God our Father in heaven and the Lord Jesus are described as merciful (*Luke* 6:36, *Heb.* 2:17). Another important element of divine mercy is revealed in the Old Testament. It is expressed in the Hebrew noun *chesed*, chiefly translated by the Greek word for mercy in the Septuagint. This focuses on God's steadfast covenant love, continually exercised towards his chosen people. In the ESV the more familiar *mercy* (AV) is rendered 'steadfast love', so that Psalm 32:10 tells us 'steadfast love surrounds the one who trusts in the LORD', and we are reminded in every verse of Psalm 136 that the steadfast love of the Lord endures forever.

The basic relevance of *peace* is that Christians have 'peace with God', and it should remind us of the solemn truth that by nature we were children of wrath and needed to be reconciled to God. The apostle frequently teaches this truth that humbles all men before God and should provoke the grateful thanks of Christians, for 'while we were enemies we were reconciled to God by the death of his Son' (*Rom.* 5:10). We are reminded also in Colossians 1:20 that Christ has made peace 'by the blood of his cross', and, since this has been accomplished, we gladly own that the believer has this peace with God as an abiding blessing which cannot be taken away nor lost. From its link with the Hebrew *shalom*, we may deduce that peace includes also the concept of spiritual prosperity, the well-being of our souls in God's secure keeping. Jesus is entitled 'Prince of Peace' (*Isa*. 9:6); he is himself our peace (*Eph*. 2:14); and in John 14:27 he comforted his disciples, 'Peace I leave with you; my peace I give to you. Let not your hearts be troubled, neither let them be afraid.' This encouragement was then extended to all Christians. In Philippians 4:6–7, Christians are exhorted:

> Do not be anxious about anything, but in everything by prayer and supplication with thanksgiving let your requests be made known to God. And the peace of God, which surpasses all understanding, will guard your hearts and your minds in Christ Jesus.

2

Timothy's Task at Ephesus

As I urged you when I was going to Macedonia, remain at Ephesus that you may charge certain persons not to teach any different doctrine, ⁴ nor to devote themselves to myths and endless genealogies, which promote speculations rather than the stewardship from God that is by faith. ⁵ The aim of our charge is love that issues from a pure heart and a good conscience and a sincere faith. ⁶ Certain persons, by swerving from these, have wandered away into vain discussion, ⁷ desiring to be teachers of the law, without understanding either what they are saying or the things about which they make confident assertions (1 Tim. 1:3–7).

We have indicated that after Paul was released from his first imprisonment in Rome he returned eventually to Philippi in Macedonia as promised (*Phil.* 2:24), and it is probable that this followed a visit to Crete where churches had been established and where he had left Titus to appoint elders who would oversee this work in every city (*Titus* 1:5). He may have revisited Ephesus in company with Timothy, though Acts 20:38, records the sorrow of the elders 'because of the word he had spoken, that they would not see his face again'. What is certain is that Timothy received this letter while in Ephesus and Paul found it necessary to urge him most strongly to remain there since there was much still to be done. Timothy was to serve the Lord there with the authority delegated by the apostle and to teach sound doctrine in order to rectify the faults and in order that the church should go forward in the right way. The church at Ephesus had been established under the three-year ministry of the apostle Paul as recorded in Acts 19, during which time, 'all the residents of Asia heard the word of the Lord, both Jews and Greeks', and, 'the word of the Lord continued to increase and prevail mightily' (*Acts* 19:10, 20). Elders had been ordained to teach and pastor the flock and when he met them at Miletus some months later Paul could claim, 'I did not shrink from declaring to you the whole counsel of God', and he urged them, 'Pay careful attention to yourselves and to all the flock, of which the Holy Spirit has made you overseers, to care for the church of God, which he obtained with his own blood' (*Acts* 20:27–28) The church had also received Paul's epistle in which he had enlarged on the glorious truths of salvation and taught that the exalted Lord Jesus, as the Head of the church, had given apostles, prophets, evangelists, pastors and teachers to build Christians up in the faith and bring them to maturity (*Eph.* 4:11–12). As 1 Timothy unfolds we find that there was need to expand instruction in this realm of the church's organized life, to correct false teaching, and to clarify the qualifications of church elders, so that unworthy men would be excluded and their influence curbed.

We have directions in this section of the letter that address the first issue. Timothy must pass on to some the word of command – this is the basic meaning of *charge* – 'not to teach any different doctrine' (verse 3). This phrase indicates that there was already a recognizable body of Christian truth, 'The faith that was once for all delivered to the saints' (*Jude* 3), and at Ephesus there were some who deviated from it to teach what we would call heresy, a different gospel from that preached by the apostles of the Lord Jesus (*Gal.* 1:8–9). The kind of error is indicated in verse 4: they gave attention to and propagated 'myths and endless genealogies, which promote speculations'.

Myths or fables are fiction in contrast with fact, and in the New Testament the word is always used contemptuously of that which is contrary to the revealed truth of God. 'We did not follow cleverly devised myths when we made known to you the power and coming of our Lord Jesus Christ, but we were eyewitnesses of his majesty' (*2 Pet.* 1:16). It is needful today to realize that there are scholars and teachers within the professing church who regard much of the narrative of the gospels as sophisticated myths, and to be careful of imbibing their teaching. The injunction of 1 John 4:1 remains relevant, 'Do not believe every spirit . . . for many false prophets have gone out into the world.' Sadly the problem of these fables remained in the church, so that it was necessary for Paul in 2 Timothy 4:4 to warn again of some who would not endure sound doctrine but would 'turn away from listening to the truth and wander off into myths'.

The *endless genealogies* referred to were probably Jewish speculations, as indicated in Titus 1:14, 'Jewish myths', legends or stories made up from them or allegorical interpretations of recorded events. Perhaps we need to reject all embellishments of biblical narrative, such as stories about Samson and Delilah, or David and Bathsheba, that appeal to lower instincts and make no contribution to upholding moral standards or supporting true doctrine. Such fictions only provoke arguments and controversies that are without any value to Christians who really need to be built up in the faith by the reliable teaching of God's revealed truth.

The phrase *stewardship from God* serves to emphasize that those who teach in Christ's church should be trustworthy stewards of God (*1 Cor.* 4:1–2, *Titus* 1:7). This may be profitably understood in the light of the solemn command of 2 Timothy 2:15, directed particularly to Timothy but relevant to all who are overseers and teachers, 'Do your best [Be diligent] to present yourself to God as one approved, a worker who has no need to be ashamed, rightly handling the word of truth.' Indeed as each Christian has received a gift from God he should use it in serving others as a good steward of God's varied grace (*1 Pet.* 4:10).

In verse 5 the positive purpose of God, what he actually commands teachers in the church to promote, is the exercise of *love* that is the fulfilment of his law (*Rom.* 13:10). The Lord Jesus employed Old Testament texts to affirm that the first and second commandments were, 'You shall love the Lord your God with all your heart and with all your soul and with all your mind and with all your strength'; and, 'You shall love your neighbour as yourself' (*Mark* 12:30–31) When love is mentioned, there is always the danger that people may deceive themselves, and to avoid this Paul teaches that Christian love has its origin in hearts that have been cleansed and renewed by the Holy Spirit. In 1 Corinthians 13:1–7 we have both an insistence on the exercise of love if one is to be regarded as a Christian and a description of its characteristics so that we may aim to conform to the Lord's standards.

The *heart* in biblical language denotes the innermost being of a person, what he really is, and especially his will that expresses itself in making decisions, and so involves both the mind and the emotions. The ability to love one another with a pure heart is traced in 1 Peter 1:22–23 to the new birth, 'since you have been born again . . . through the living and abiding word of God'. It is characteristic of Christ's disciples: 'Blessed are the pure in heart' (*Matt.* 5:8). This requirement is enlarged on in 2 Timothy 2:22: 'Pursue righteousness, faith, love, and peace along with those who call on the Lord from a pure heart.'

Conscience is a faculty that God has implanted in men by which we can read God's law written in our hearts (*Rom.* 2:15), but sin has marred its functioning so that it needs the blood of Christ to make it work effectively. One of the sad facts of modern society is that it not only has departed from scriptural teaching of right and wrong but also suggests that there is no absolute standard of goodness. Many have a defective or defiled conscience (*Titus* 1:15), one that has been made insensitive as if cauterized, so that it does not respond to moral stimuli (*1 Tim.* 4:2), but we should aim like Paul to serve God with a pure conscience (*2 Tim.* 1:3). Because of its defects and limitations conscience must be informed and regulated by the Word of God if we are to discern and practise what is right, and we must recognize and emphasize that God himself alone is Lord of the conscience.

Sincere faith is here contrasted with a mere profession of faith that is hypocritical – a matter of pretence like actors in a play who adopt another character – and this was the fault of many Pharisees in Jesus' time whom he often accused of being hypocrites. They tended to concentrate on outward conformity to traditional rules and regulations that were not determined from God's Word, and he told them, 'You . . . have neglected the weightier matters of the law: justice and mercy and faithfulness' (*Matt.* 23:23).

As in Ephesus then, so today there are many who profess to be Christians who need to be challenged about the reality and sincerity of their faith often because they have not understood what it really means to be a Christian. The exercise of true faith is only possible when God has made people alive and saved them by his grace. It cannot be derived merely from parentage or church background or human instruction. All need to consider the relevance of Paul's requirement in 2 Corinthians 13:5, 'Examine yourselves, to see whether you are in the faith.' Christian love can only emanate from a renewed and cleansed heart, informed and motivated by a good, active conscience, as evidence of sincere faith that works by love.

Those who taught a different doctrine had missed the mark of God's purpose in His commandment and had turned aside from it and devoted themselves instead to futile talk by which others too could be led astray from God's path of life. Paul had warned the Ephesian elders, 'From among your own selves will arise men speaking twisted things, to draw away the disciples after them' (*Acts* 20:30).

These men were guilty of selfish ambition, wanting to have the reputation of being 'Law Teachers', though they utterly failed to understand what they were actually teaching and the things they strongly affirmed. We are reminded of the description of the false teachers mentioned in 2 Peter 2:18 who spoke loud boasts of folly. In Jude 16 they are called 'loud-mouthed boasters'. Despite their arrogant boasts they were ignorant of the true nature and design of God's law and even used terminology that was beyond their comprehension. Though they professed to teach the law of God given by Moses they had no real understanding of the principles of conduct that God required.

3

The Proper Use of God's Law

Now we know that the law is good if one uses it lawfully,
⁹ understanding this, that the law is not laid down for the just
but for the lawless and disobedient, for the ungodly and sinners,
for the unholy and profane, for those who strike their fathers
and mothers, for murderers, ¹⁰ the sexually immoral, men who
practise homosexuality, enslavers, liars, perjurers, and what-
ever else is contrary to sound doctrine, ¹¹ in accordance with
the glorious gospel of the blessed God with which I have been
entrusted (1 Tim. 1:8–11).

The exposure of the misunderstanding and misuse of the law is followed by this insistence on its real value and place in Christian teaching, for the law is excellent and perfectly suited to God's purpose, provided that it is used lawfully, that is, according to his design. Paul explains in Romans 7:13 that the law is good because by it the sinfulness of sin is revealed, and it thereby serves as a schoolmaster or child-trainer to bring men to Christ (*Gal.* 3:24). We should not regard the law merely in terms of the specific commandments, for the basic Hebrew term *Torah* more widely includes all divine revelation to guide human conduct. Here then we recognize a reference to all God's instructions, not only as they were revealed by Moses, but also as they were developed by the prophets and subsequently embodied in the Old Testament Scriptures. The law was not made for a righteous person but was given in the context of human sinfulness for, in God's esteem, 'None is righteous, no, not one' (*Rom.* 3:10).

This does not mean, however, that the law does not relate to those who are reckoned righteous by God, for it contains his direction for their lives and, as their Father, he wants obedient children (*1 Pet.* 1:14). John Calvin notes two benefits that Christians derive from the law. 'It is the best instrument for enabling them daily to learn with greater truth and certainty what that will of the Lord is which they aspire to follow . . . By frequently meditating upon it [God's servant] will be excited to obedience and confirmed in it' (*Institutes,* Book II, ch. 7, sect. 12)

The catalogue of sinful attitudes and activities in verses 9–11 generally reflects the order of the Ten Commandments, since the first four identify offences directly against God himself and the remaining six those against our fellow men. The words used to describe the unrighteous are almost self-explanatory but a little clarification may prove helpful.

Men who are *lawless and disobedient* both disregard God's law and actively violate it by rejecting his claim on their total obedience as Lawgiver and Judge.

The *ungodly* lack reverence for God; they are those described in Psalm 36:1, quoted in Romans 3:18, 'There is no fear of God before their eyes.'

The simple descriptive word *sinners* is a more familiar and comprehensive term that reiterates the solemn fact that, 'All have sinned and fall short of the glory of God' (*Rom.* 3:23).

Unholy persons are those who lack true piety; they are not loyally devoted to God in worship and service and are also termed *profane* because nothing is sacred to them. They lack any real concern to honour the holiness of God's name and the sanctity of his ordinances, which would include his command, 'Remember the Sabbath day, to keep it holy' (*Exod.* 20:8).

The breach of any of these first four commandments is clearly a failure to obey the summary commandment referred to in verse 5 that we should love God with all our faculties, by expending our energies and employing our time to please him.

The following offences reveal failure to obey what is often called, 'The Second Table of the Law'. It can be summarized, 'You shall love your neighbour as yourself' (see James 2:8, where it is called, 'The royal law according to the Scripture').

The first element mentioned is the extreme expression of disregard of God's requirement that we should honour our fathers

[13]

and mothers. The translation in the ESV is more accurate than the expression 'murderers of parents', for the verb used basically means to smite or use a cudgel, and the offence of beating one's parent is mentioned in Exodus 21:15 and there declared to deserve the death penalty.

The serious nature of the sin of *murder* is indicated in Genesis 9:6, where it is said that it deserves the death penalty, for it is the shedding of the blood of a fellow human being who was made in the image of God.

God's command, 'You shall not commit adultery', is broken both by heterosexual activity outside of marriage and by all homosexual practices. The fact that such vile practices were so prevalent among the inhabitants of Sodom in the days of Lot has given rise to the older term 'Sodomites', which serves to recall the fact that it brought God's destruction (*Gen.* 19:5,24). This was an example of the vengeance of eternal fire (*Jude* 7) and so highlights the seriousness of this sin. God's design in what we may term the procreative impulse, more popularly called the sex-drive, is that a man and woman should become one in marriage and have children whom they may nurture for God in the bond of the family relationship (*Mal.* 2:15). We must glorify God in this use of our bodies, for the body is not for sexual immorality but for the Lord (*1 Cor.* 6:12,20). In recent years Western society has become increasingly tolerant of this breach of divine law. To contend for God's teaching in this realm is a necessary though uphill battle for the Christian and could result in the experience of the state's disapproval through its legal system. The teaching of God's Word is transparently explicit: homosexual activity is yielding to a debased mind and vile passions and committing what is shameful (*Rom.* 1:26–28), and those who are guilty of it have no place in the Christian church. However, they are not a hopeless class of sinners; the exalted Saviour may give them repentance and forgiveness of sins (*Acts* 5:31). And in fact some have been saved, as recorded in 1 Corinthians 6:11: 'Such were some of you. But you were washed, you were sanctified, you were justified in the name of the Lord Jesus Christ and by the Spirit of our God.'

Enslavers would include those we call 'kidnappers', and obviously denotes those who forcibly deprive men of their liberty, including selling them into slavery. The seriousness of this most repulsive violation of the eighth commandment is manifest by its condemnation in Exodus 21:17 and Deuteronomy 24:7, as a sin worthy of death. Sadly the practice of slave-making has not completely ceased; but besides criticism of it, as Christians we should pray for those suffering from it, for many of our brothers and sisters in Christ are included.

It may surprise us to find *liars* in this list of gross sinners since in modern times lying has become almost a way of life for some who are concerned for their position or reputation. The *Observer* newspaper of 29 December 1974 included among the 'Sayings of the Year', these words: 'In our country the lie has become not just a moral category but a pillar of the state.' Some would minimize its sinfulness and describe it merely as being economical with the truth, but God's Word here, as regularly, most strongly condemns the practice of telling lies. The Lord Jesus Christ described the devil as 'a liar and the father of lies' (*John* 8:44), and there is the warning in Revelation 22:15 that 'everyone who loves and practises falsehood' will be excluded from the New Jerusalem. God is offended by all lying and those who commit perjury have more greatly insulted him by misusing his name as if they called on him as a witness to their integrity, particularly when they swear on the Bible. The offence of perjury is the deliberate telling of a lie in a court of law when one has sworn to be truthful.

It would be impossible to give a comprehensive lists of all sinful attitudes and acts, so here Paul sums them up as all other things that are contrary to sound doctrine. This is the first occurrence of this phrase denoting teaching that is pure from error and that will promote the healthy growth of Christians. The whole of the Christian's life ought to adorn the doctrine of God our Saviour in all things and all blemishes of character and breaches of his law are failures to do so and tend to bring dishonour to his holy name.

Paul concludes this section by his claim that what he had taught about the proper use of the law was in accord with the gospel, for there is no minimizing of God's standards of acceptable conduct in the fresh revelation of the New Testament. The Greek expression in verse 11 is more exactly translated, 'the gospel of the glory of the blessed God', and indicates that the gospel reveals the glory of God in our salvation and is the means by which God has shone into our hearts to give the light of the knowledge of his glory in the face of Jesus Christ (*2 Cor.* 4:6).

The description *blessed* is only used of God here and in 1 Timothy 6:15. It serves to emphasize his essential perfections, his transcendent goodness, and his self-sufficient happiness. The glory of God here relates to the revelation of the glory of his grace in the work of salvation (*Eph.* 1:6). This enables those justified by grace to rejoice in the hope of the glory of God (*Rom.* 5:1–2).

Already believers have seen the glory of the only-begotten Son (*John* 1:14), and wait for the appearing of the glory of our great God and Saviour Jesus Christ (*Titus* 2:13).

Paul indicates his sense of great privilege that he has been entrusted with this gospel, as later of his discharge of the responsibility: 'Just as we have been approved by God to be entrusted with the gospel, so we speak, not to please man, but to please God who tests our hearts' (*1 Thess.* 2:4).

4

Paul's Thanksgiving to God for His Abundant Grace

I thank him who has given me strength, Christ Jesus our Lord, because he judged me faithful, appointing me to his service, ¹³ though formerly I was a blasphemer, persecutor, and insolent opponent. But I received mercy because I had acted ignorantly in unbelief, ¹⁴ and the grace of our Lord overflowed for me with the faith and love that are in Christ Jesus. ¹⁵ The saying is trustworthy and deserving of full acceptance, that Christ Jesus came into the world to save sinners, of whom I am the foremost. ¹⁶ But I received mercy for this reason, that in me as the foremost, Jesus Christ might display his perfect patience as an example to those who were to believe in him for eternal life. ¹⁷ To the King of ages, immortal, invisible, the only God, be honour and glory for ever and ever. Amen (1 Tim. 1:12–17).

Paul continues with thanks to Christ Jesus, whom he calls 'our Lord', for the great privilege and honour of being a minister of the gospel, since this came about according to the gift of the grace of God, given to him by the working of God's power, given that he should preach the unsearchable riches of Christ (*Eph.* 3:7–8). It was God who made him, as he makes other faithful ministers of the New Covenant, competent or sufficient for the discharge of this office (*2 Cor.* 3:5–6); as he attests here, Christ Jesus empowered him.

The verb translated 'has given me strength' can be linked with the promise of Jesus to his disciples in Acts 1:8, 'You will receive power when the Holy Spirit has come upon you and you will be my witnesses.' Earlier Paul, using the same verb, had written in Ephesians 6:10, 'Be strong in the Lord and in the strength of his might', in order to engage in Christian warfare, and later he wrote to Timothy, 'Be strengthened by the grace that is in Christ Jesus' (2 Tim. 2:1). We should be encouraged that the Lord will always give enabling power to all those whom he has called to be his disciples in order that they may serve him in their different roles and responsibilities.

Christ had reckoned that Paul would be *faithful* or trustworthy when he put him into his service (verse 12). Before Festus and Agrippa he could claim, 'I was not disobedient to the heavenly vision' (*Acts* 26:19), and in the prospect of death in 2 Timothy 4:7 he wrote, 'I have kept the faith.'

Paul then relates his gratitude to Christ Jesus to his utter unworthiness of this great privilege because of his past way of life. He had been a *blasphemer* (verse 13), denying that Jesus of Nazareth was the promised Messiah and the Son of God, and had both spoken and acted against him, even trying to make others blaspheme (*Acts* 26:11). His *persecution* of believers is reported in the Acts of the Apostles (*Acts* 8:3, 9:1), and when the Lord Jesus appeared to him on the Damascus road he asked him, 'Saul, Saul, why are you persecuting me?'

An *insolent opponent* (verse 13) is one who both speaks with contempt and acts outrageously, and Jesus had prophesied that he himself would be treated in such a cruel manner (*Luke* 18:32). Paul here owns up to being such a grievous sinner, and yet one who had received mercy, and as this truth is repeated in verse 16 we can imagine how his heart freshly overflowed in adoring praise of his Saviour at the recollection of it.

The clause, 'because I had acted ignorantly in unbelief', is not an attempt to minimize his guiltiness, because neither ignorance nor unbelief could excuse his hostility to the Lord Jesus Christ and his disciples. The amazing extent of divine mercy that he experienced reminds us of the the prayer of Jesus while he was hanging on the cross, 'Father, forgive them, for they know not what they do' (*Luke* 23:34), and this provides a basis for real hope not only to those directly responsible for his death but to all who have previously ignored him in unbelief of his claims to be the Son of God and the anointed Saviour.

[18]

The first element of the work of the Holy Spirit is to convince men of sin because they do not believe in the Lord Jesus (*John* 16:8–9), and he is pleased to accomplish this by the preaching of the gospel, as demonstrated in Acts 2:37–41.

The apostle struggles to find an adequate way of expressing the amazing grace of our Lord in his conversion and here uses a compound verb that means 'superabounded' (*overflowed* in the ESV rendering). It passed the boundary of human comprehension and was unparalleled in human experience. There is a near equivalent in Romans 5:20, 'Where sin abounded, grace abundantly overflowed' (my translation). John Bunyan acknowledges this experience well in his autobiography, *Grace Abounding to the Chief of Sinners*, as he recounts the Lord's gracious dealings with him.

The effect of this abundant grace in Paul's experience was his own exercise of *faith and love* in union with Christ. *Faith* is an obvious contrast with previous unbelief, and *love* with the former hostility that he had showed to the Lord Jesus, and this shows, as Calvin said, 'God had so completely changed him, that he had become a totally different and new man.' If any one is in Christ he is a new creation and has put on the new man created according to God, and indeed, like Paul, has become a new 'man in Christ' (*2 Cor.* 5:17; 12:2, and *Eph.* 4:24)

Paul continues to write about the Lord's saving grace to him by connecting it directly to the purpose of his mission as Saviour and introduces it with an emphasis upon the perfect trustworthiness and universal relevance of this saying (verses 15–16). The brief clause, 'The saying is trustworthy', is found four more times in the Pastoral Epistles (*1 Tim.* 3:1, 4:9; *2 Tim.* 2:11; *Titus* 3:8). It has often been assumed, though it has not been proved, that he thereby affixes the seal of apostolic authority to a truth already well known among Christians, but its presence here adequately confirms that it belongs within the divine revelation of Holy Scripture. Besides being a *trustworthy*, that is, an utterly reliable word from God, this saying is worthy of the welcoming acceptance of all men without any hesitation or reservation.

This familiar text is a brief summary of the essence of the Christian gospel and well repays a closer examination. Christ Jesus is identified with the Son of God who in time, according to the divine purpose, came into the world from heaven, taking human nature from the womb of the virgin Mary, so that he now is both true God and true man, one Person with these two natures.

The record of the gospels according to Matthew and Luke is enhanced by the testimony of John 1:14, 'The Word became flesh and dwelt among us, and we have seen his glory, glory as of the only Son from the Father.' The condescension and self-humbling involved in the incarnation are also described in Philippians 2:6–8: the One who was essentially God made himself of no reputation and took the form of a servant and was obedient even to the death of the cross. His purpose in coming into the world was to save sinners, as Jesus himself had taught, 'The Son of Man came to seek and to save the lost' (*Luke* 19:10). This salvation included their rescue from the power of sin and the penalty of sin, and was accomplished by his death: 'In him we have redemption through his blood, the forgiveness of our trespasses, according to the riches of his grace' (*Eph.* 1:7). All who realize that they are sinners should rejoice that this simple gospel truth is relevant to them and so be encouraged to repent of their sins and embrace the Lord Jesus in the arms of faith. That is precisely what Paul had done and personally invited the Philippian jailer to do when he was concerned about salvation: 'Believe in the Lord Jesus, and you will be saved' (*Acts* 16:31).

Since Paul considered himself the chief or *foremost* sinner and yet had obtained mercy, this fact should encourage even the worst of men to seek that divine mercy for themselves. Indeed he writes of himself as one in whom God had clearly demonstrated the wonderful extent of his longsuffering, a pattern of its greatness, so that those who are deeply convicted of their sinfulness might similarly believe on the Lord Jesus to receive eternal life.

We should note that Paul still held this low view of himself as the foremost of sinners, for he does not say, 'I was', but, 'I am', and his comments in Romans 7:24–25 reflect this, 'Wretched man that I am! Who will deliver me from this body of death? Thanks be to God through Jesus Christ our Lord!'

Paul's thanksgiving for God's grace begun in verse 12 is now concluded in reverent adoration, ascribing honour and glory to God (verse 17), and our study should promote our own grateful response to our God.

The expression, 'King eternal' (AV/NKJV) is more literally translated as *King of ages*, a concept found frequently in the Old Testament, though not in these terms. In Psalm 90:2 Moses declares, 'From everlasting to everlasting you are God', and in Exodus 15:18, 'The LORD will reign for ever and ever.' David also praised the LORD in Psalm 145, and in verse 13 testified, 'Your kingdom is an everlasting kingdom, and your dominion endures throughout all generations', an understanding to which God brought Nebuchadnezzar (*Dan.* 4:34). It is because God is the supreme ruler over all human history that we may be assured that he works all things according to the counsel of his will, and for the good of those who love him (*Eph.* 1:11, *Rom.* 8:28).

The affirmation that God is *immortal* or incorruptible not only teaches us that he is without sin but also that he is not subject to change nor liable to death. In Romans 1:23 the only other use of this adjective emphasizes that the great folly of those who rejected God's self-revelation was to exchange the glory of the immortal God for images made like mortal man and other creatures. In Malachi 3:6, God declares, 'I the LORD do not change.' Similarly, it is said in James 1:17 that with God, the Father of lights, there is no variation or shadow due to change. This truth is the foundation of the confidence of God's people.

God is also *invisible* in his own being. He cannot be seen by the human eye, as we are taught in John 1:18 and 1 John 4:12: 'No one has ever seen God.' We can only know God as he is pleased to reveal himself, which he did firstly by means of his Word, but then supremely and fully in his only-begotten Son, the Lord Jesus Christ. So Christ is described as 'the image of the invisible God' (*Col.* 1:15), and in John 14:9 he declared to Philip, 'Whoever has seen me has seen the Father.'

Because there were many gods and many lords in the contemporary religious world (*1 Cor.* 8:5), it is next insisted that he is *the only God*, as had been taught repeatedly in the Old Testament. 'The LORD is God in heaven above and on the earth beneath; there is no other' (*Deut.* 4:39). He created the heavens and the earth and claims, 'I am the LORD, and there is no other . . . there is no other god besides me' (*Isa.* 45:18, 21). In ascribing glory to God in Romans 16:26–27, Paul had described him as the eternal God and the only God, and there he added the adjective 'wise'; but though it is certain that God is uniquely wise, it is not so certain that that fact is asserted in 1 Timothy 1:17, for the word 'wise' is absent from most early manuscripts.

This truth that he alone is the true God underlies the contrast made with false, unreal gods in 1 Thessalonians 1:9, by the statement that believers there 'turned to God from idols to serve the living and true God', and in Acts 14:15 idolaters were exhorted to turn from the useless futilities of false gods to the living God who made the heaven and the earth.

Honour and glory belong to our God, and therefore we ought to honour him by our obedience to his Word in worship and service, with the over-riding concern always that God will be glorified in all things. We cannot add to his glory, but we should declare his glory to the nations (*Psa*. 96:3), and by our reverence to him as our God we can encourage others also to glorify him. Such adoring praise and worship is given to the God who lives for ever and ever in Revelation 4:11, 'Worthy are you, our Lord and God, to receive glory and honour and power, for you created all things, and by your will they existed and were created.' Paul is frequently concerned to ascribe glory to God, as in Romans 11:33, 36, 'Oh, the depth of the riches and wisdom and knowledge of God! . . . For from him and through him and to him are all things. To him be glory for ever. Amen' (see also *Phil*. 4:20, *2 Tim*. 4:18). The exhortation of Revelation 14:7, 'Fear God and give him glory', is a permanent guide to our responsibility. This is summed up in the *Westminster Larger Catechism*, Answer 1: 'Man's chief and highest end is to glorify God, and fully to enjoy him for ever.'

5

Paul's Solemn Charge to Timothy

*This charge I entrust to you, Timothy, my child, in accordance with
the prophecies previously made about you, that by them you may
wage the good warfare, ¹⁹ holding faith and a good conscience. By
rejecting this some have made shipwreck of their faith, ²⁰ among whom
are Hymenaeus and Alexander, whom I have handed over to Satan
that they may learn not to blaspheme* (1 Tim. 1:18–20).

Paul here reinforces his earlier charge to Timothy that he should
command others not to teach any doctrine different from the
truths previously declared to them under his apostolic authority.
God's declared purpose in verse 5 was that the lives of Christians
should be characterized by 'love that issues from a pure heart and
a good conscience and a sincere faith', but sadly some had already
rejected it. In committing this vital task to Timothy, Paul tenderly
addresses him as a son in the faith, so conjoining his apostolic
authority with this relevant personal relationship, in order that
Timothy should both receive it as a sacred trust and at the same
time regard Paul as a spiritual mentor.

This duty, however, was nothing newly imposed but was in
accord with the prophecies that had attended Timothy, probably
on the solemn occasion of his ordination, when the Holy Spirit had
borne testimony to his future life's work. We understand that this
had included the laying on of the hands of Paul (*2 Tim.* 1:6), and
of the council of elders (*1 Tim.* 4:14), and if, as seems most likely,
Silas was among those elders (for he had accompanied Paul to Lystra), the prophecy may have come through him, for he was called a
prophet in Acts 15:32. This event then was like the involvement of
prophets in the setting apart of Barnabas and Saul for the first missionary journey. Then the Holy Spirit told the church leaders at

Antioch, 'Set apart for me Barnabas and Saul for the work to which I have called them', so that they were 'sent out by the Holy Spirit' (*Acts* 13:3–4). By this divinely-given endorsement of his call to the ministry Timothy would doubtless have been greatly encouraged to discharge his task despite the potential problems and the real difficulties soon encountered. We may here note Paul's words in 2 Timothy 1:6–7, 'I remind you to fan into flame the gift of God, which is in you through the laying on of my hands, for God gave us a spirit not of fear but of power and love and self control.'

This work to which God had called him was one of continual spiritual *warfare* and was to be fought in accord with and in the strength of those prophecies. It required Timothy as a good soldier of Jesus Christ to endure hardship so as to please the Lord who enlisted him. Paul had earlier exhorted all Christians to engage in this conflict: 'Put on the whole armour of God' (*Eph.* 6:10–11). That included taking up the shield of faith and the sword of the Spirit, which is the Word of God. Timothy and all church leaders, pastors and teachers have a prominent role and must be extra vigilant in all aspects of this warfare. By their teaching of the truth they should greatly assist every believer, for all are inescapably involved and must engage positively and personally in it. They all may and should fight their battles with confidence because, as Paul has written, 'The weapons of our warfare are not of the flesh but have divine power to destroy strongholds' (*2 Cor.* 10:4).

It is vitally important that in the conduct of this excellent warfare Timothy, and every minister, should continue to *hold faith* (verse 19), probably meaning faith in the sound doctrine, and the *good conscience* that God requires, as already mentioned in verse 5. John Calvin has well expressed this:

> The chief things demanded from a teacher are these two: that he shall hold by the pure truth of the gospel; and, next, that he shall administer it with a good conscience and honest zeal.

It is an abiding duty incumbent on all believers to contend earnestly for the faith once delivered to them in the holy Scriptures (*Jude* 3), and those whom God has put into the ministry must preach the Word to equip and encourage them in this demanding task (*2 Tim.* 3:16–4:2). Timothy was associated with Paul in the writing of 2 Corinthians and the testimony of chapter 4:1–2 is a guide to their practice:

> Therefore, having this ministry by the mercy of God, we do not lose heart. But we have renounced disgraceful, underhanded ways. We refuse to practise cunning or to tamper with God's word, but by the open statement of the truth we would commend ourselves to everyone's conscience in the sight of God.

Earlier in that letter, Paul included Timothy when he wrote of the testimony of his conscience, 'We behaved in the world with simplicity and godly sincerity, not by earthly wisdom but by the grace of God and supremely so towards you' (*2 Cor.* 1:12). Timothy must aim to maintain that testimony.

Like Paul, we all should take pains to have a clear conscience towards both God and man in all things (*Acts* 24:16), so that our behaviour commends the doctrine of God our Saviour and does not incur the fair criticism of unbelievers (*1 Pet.* 3:16).

A good conscience is one that is alert, works efficiently in accord with God's standards, and is continually being enlightened and informed by the Holy Spirit, through one's meditation on the Word of God. Where it produces conviction of failure in the moral realm or in relation to our service of God there should be confession and amendment so that God may renew the joy of salvation and make us cleaner vessels, more fit for the Master's use.

God alone is Lord of the conscience and he uses it in conjunction with his Word of truth to reveal the true state of our hearts before him, so that, as Calvin said, 'A good conscience is nothing else than integrity of heart' (*Institutes*, Book III, ch. 19, sect. 16).

Some had already pushed aside the claims of conscience and had shut their ears against God's voice and so suffered *shipwreck* in their faith (verse 20). The invaluable treasure of Christian doctrine must always be securely guarded by an active divinely-informed conscience, and when a man deviates from the safe course God has charted, then great loss will follow, here likened to a shipwreck. A bad and insensitive conscience will lead to the embrace of false doctrines and to the abandoning of Christian morality, which will result in the destruction of faith. This warning ought to be carefully observed by all professing Christians.

We may think of conscience as the helmsman of the ship that carries the cargo of *the faith*. When his voice is not heeded, the ship will go off course and be wrecked on the rocks and the cargo will be lost overboard.

The history of the Christian church contains many sad evidences of this failure, and here Paul names two who had deviated from the truth and abandoned vital elements of Christianity.

Hymenaus is mentioned again in 2 Timothy 2:17 as one guilty of irreverent babble which led people into more and more ungodliness. The particular way in which he had turned aside from the truth was in saying that the resurrection was already past. The seriousness of false teaching in this realm was dealt with in 1 Corinthians 15 where the fact of the resurrection of the Lord Jesus Christ is established as the foundation of the future resurrection that will take place when he comes again in power and glory. Error about the resurrection will necessarily affect conduct. Keeping company with those who hold it will ruin good morals (*1 Cor.* 15:33).

Such false teaching is likened to cancer or gangrene (*2 Tim.* 2:17) which, if unchecked, will spread through the whole body of the church. Its propagators must not only be silenced but also removed from any office and excommunicated to preserve Christians from the likely spiritual harm. The failure of Christian churches to exercise such scriptural discipline has through the centuries led to the dissemination of false teaching and caused their weakening under divine judgment.

When the church tolerates those who teach false doctrine and who may even claim prophetic status she incurs the severe displeasure of the exalted Lord Jesus who searches the hearts and the minds (*Rev.* 2:14, 20). This should serve to warn all of us against the reading of material that openly or more subtly advocates doctrinal or moral error, lest we be tempted by it to compromise our biblically-based convictions. There is a real danger that we might over-confidently regard ourselves as invulnerable to such a failing, so that we greatly need to respond to the warning, 'Let anyone who thinks that he stands take heed lest he fall' (*1 Cor.* 10:12), and rely only on God's faithfulness as our safeguard.

It is probable that besides excommunication, which is an action performed by the church, the words of Paul here refer to the exercise of his apostolic authority to hand a person over to Satan's power for the affliction of his body, as in 1 Corinthians 5:5. Many commentators share the view that by this act Hymenaeus, and his co-heretic Alexander, were removed from church membership and subjected to some physical illness as a mark of divine displeasure. (Because Alexander was such a common name, it seems impossible to identify him with any degree of certainty, either with the man of that name in Ephesus [*Acts* 19:33], or the coppersmith in Rome [*2 Tim.* 4:14].)

This very severe punishment was not merely negative but had a positive design, that those punished should be educated by such discipline to renounce error and cease blaspheming. We note that the purpose of the treatment of the offender against Christian morality in 1 Corinthians 5:5, had a similar intent, for it was 'so that his spirit may be saved in the day of the Lord'. It must always be insisted that the exercise of church discipline should only take place under the clear scriptural command of the Lord Jesus Christ, the Head of the church, for his honour, to promote the welfare of his church, and with the prayerful hope that the sinner might be restored. This will reflect the kindly invitation of the Lord to Israel, when as a nation guilty of both heresy and schism he called her to return to him, with the encouragement, 'I will heal their backsliding (ESV: *apostasy*); I will love them freely' (*Hos.* 14:4).

6

Public Prayer in the
Worshipping Congregation

First of all then, I urge that supplications, prayers, intercessions, and thanksgivings be made for all people, ² for kings and all who are in high positions, that we may lead a peaceful and quiet life, godly and dignified in every way. ³ This is good and it is pleasing in the sight of God our Saviour, ⁴ who desires all people to be saved and to come to the knowledge of the truth. ⁵ For there is one God and there is one mediator between God and men, the man Christ Jesus, who gave himself a ransom for all, which is the testimony given at the proper time. ⁷ For this I was appointed a preacher and an apostle (I am telling the truth, I am not lying), a teacher of the Gentiles in faith and truth (1 Tim. 2:1–7).

In Chapter 2 we enter into one of the major concerns of the apostle in this letter: to provide needed vital instruction for the ordering of the life and the worship of the Christian church that would retain its God-given authority through the centuries.

It must always be emphasized that the Lord Jesus Christ is the Head of the church and that he rules her by means of the holy Scriptures. Individual believers and also congregations should gladly and lovingly obey him by endeavouring to conform to the pattern that he has provided in the Scriptures. Submission to our Lord and Saviour ought always to be a delightful priority and Christians show this by recognizing and implementing the evangelical and Reformed conviction that is termed *the regulative principle of Scripture*.

Martin Luther expressed this in his commentary on Galatians 1:8–9:

> Paul subjects himself and all other teachers and masters under
> the authority of the Scripture. This queen ought to rule and all
> ought to obey and be subject unto her, and be only witnesses,
> disciples and confessors of the Scripture.

In these days it seems that this fundamental principle is not insisted on, perhaps not even considered, in many congregations, so
that the teaching of the apostle Paul may come as a shock and promote some heart-searching. We should remember however that it
was also needed in the first century, for Paul wrote with the knowledge of the situation at Ephesus that would be replicated in later
centuries. Our responsibility is simply to affirm that the Lord Jesus
Christ knows what is best for his church and thus, with due humility, submit to his guidance for her greatest good.

It is surely significant that Paul does not begin with what we
would call church order but with this theme of the church's corporate prayer life, a priority that must not be forgotten or overlooked if we wish to be scriptural.

Though the verb in verse 1 may properly be translated 'urge' or
'exhort' or 'encourage', the introductory *then* links this directly to
the apostolic authority that was claimed in the first chapter. If we
want to please God our Saviour, and Christ Jesus our hope, we will
welcome these directions concerning prayer, as the disciples, aware
of their needs, asked, 'Lord, teach us to pray' (*Luke* 11:1). It is
plain from Matthew 6 that the Lord Jesus expected his disciples to
pray, as he repeated, 'When you pray' (*Matt.* 6:5–7), before giving
them both a pattern for prayer (*Matt.* 6:9–13) and encouragements
to pray (*Matt.* 7:7–11). We should be glad that we have such a
guide, for often we do not know how to pray, and so can profit from
this teaching about the ingredients or distinct aspects of prayer.
Although the exhortation is concerned with prayer in the congregation, there is obviously much here to help all believers

We must humbly take our place before God as those who are
totally dependent on him and acknowledge our insufficiency by
making specific requests, *supplications*, or petitions, according to
our many and varied needs as a church and as individual members.
Christians are encouraged to come because God is their heavenly
Father, knows to give good gifts to his children, and is well able
to meet our needs.

John Newton gave helpful guidance in this:

> Thou art coming to a King;
> Large petitions with thee bring;
> For his grace and power are such,
> None can ever ask too much.

The most comprehensive term is *prayers,* though it is signifi-cant that its usage in the Scriptures is confined to addressing God, whereas petitions may be employed towards men. It emphasizes the element of devotion, drawing near to God with reverence to enjoy fellowship with him, not merely to obtain some benefit from him! In prayer we commit ourselves and our cause, here especially the welfare of the church, to God, since we realize that a vital part of our Christian warfare is to pray at all times with every kind of prayer and supplication in the Spirit (*Eph.* 6:18).

Intercessions are earnest pleadings with God, though they extend beyond the normal restrictive concept of the term, as is apparent in 1 Timothy 4:5, where the noun is simply translated *prayer.* In secular Greek the word was commonly used simply for petitions to a superior, but its derivation suggests the idea of meeting together for conversation, so that for the Christian it would denote the en-joyment of free access to God through the Lord Jesus in union with the Holy Spirit (*Eph.* 2:18). The Holy Spirit himself has been given to help us in our weakness and ignorance in this realm and he himself makes intercessions for the saints according to the will of God (*Rom.* 8:26–27).

The meaning of *thanksgivings* is most obvious, but its impor-tance is frequently overlooked because the ingratitude that was often found in Israel is still prevalent today. We ought to stir up our minds to recall God's mercies to us, supremely of course in our own salvation and the spiritual blessings that are ours in Christ, but also in all the affairs of our normal life in the world. Such grateful acknowledgement of God's kind dealings with us is commended in Ephesians 5:20, 'Giving thanks always and for everything to God the Father in the name of our Lord Jesus Christ'. Thanksgiving is to be part of our prayers, as the remedy for anxiety given in Philip-pians 4:6 shows, for every grateful remembrance of God's previous giving encourages us to ask for more.

These varied elements in the exercise of prayer should have the widest scope: *for all people*, perhaps meaning all kinds of men, 'all sorts and conditions of men', as the *Book of Common Prayer* puts it. Though our fellow believers must occupy an important place in our prayers as indicated in the Lord's Prayer where we find the plurals *us* and *our*, prayer must not be restricted to the family of God. The command to love our neighbours as ourselves was endorsed by Jesus (*Mark* 12:31), and surely must include prayer on their behalf, especially but not exclusively for their spiritual welfare. In addition, it was the Lord Jesus who said to his disciples, 'Pray for those who persecute you' (*Matt.* 5:44).

We have particular mention in verse 2 of those with authority in society. Whether they be hereditary monarchs, dictators, or democratically elected rulers, it remains a Christian responsibility to pray for them.

So often we can feel helpless when rulers set aside biblical standards for public life and introduce laws in direct conflict with them, since we believe that righteousness exalts a nation and that sin is a reproach to any people (*Prov.* 14:34), but the remedy is in prayer to the Almighty God who rules over all. E. K. Simpson has this fine comment:

> The supplication of faithful intercessors for the common weal [welfare] lays invisible restraints on the powers of darkness and their tools, and brings reinforcement to honest rulers from the Governor among the nations.

We may learn from the Lord's command to the Jews when in exile (*Jer.* 29:7), 'Seek the welfare of the city [Babylon] . . . and pray to the LORD on its behalf', and we should recall that when Paul wrote the Christian church was suffering at the hands of Jewish and Roman authorities.

The stated aim of these prayers is that Christians may benefit from the law and order of stable political government, and the adjectives *peaceful and quiet* denote both the tranquillity that is enjoyed when freed from external pressures and the serenity that comes from within. There is a relevant record in Acts 9:31, 'The church . . . had peace, and was being built up. And walking in the fear of the Lord and in the comfort of the Holy Spirit, it multiplied.'

[31]

However, when God does answer prayer to ease the pressures on Christians it is not to promote their material prosperity or induce carelessness, for that would be an abuse of God's providential kindness. We ought rather to be concerned for growth in godliness by using as fully as possible all the public means of grace available to us that are denied to believers under oppressive regimes, and exercising our responsibilities to be Christ's witnesses.

The second noun, represented in the ESV by *dignified,* is variously translated; AV: *honesty*, NKJV: *reverence*, NIV: *holiness*; and, since it is linked with a verb meaning 'to worship', it may even denote *veneration.* The changes made in believers' lives should produce in them a quality of seriousness that is not marred by flippancy or crude joking but deserves respect.

The best reason for any activity, whether in the worship of God or in daily life, is that it meets with God's approval and, recognizing that the command to pray in this manner originated with God, we may be assured of this. There is intrinsic comeliness even excellence in such praying, for the adjective *good* carries this meaning. Jesus used it in this way in describing himself as the Good Shepherd, one who is proficient in shepherding. It is not merely acceptable to God when his children respond to his invitation to draw near in prayer but he welcomes them and takes pleasure in their fellowship and their expression of dependence on him.

As we noted in 1 Timothy 1:1, God the Father is also here designated as *God our Saviour*, reminding us that he rules over all as our kind and caring Benefactor, as well as being the source of our salvation from sin.

We are here taught that God *desires all people to be saved* (verse 4) and since there has been much contention about its precise meaning it is probably wise, if not necessary, to consider the different elements of the statement. It does not mean that it is God's determined will that every man should be saved, for it is plain from many passages of Scriptures that some will be punished for their sins and be excluded from heaven. The phrase *all people* may properly denote all kinds of men, in accord with normal Greek usage, and certainly cannot be pressed to mean every human being that has ever lived. However the verse does express his revealed will in accord with his words in Ezekiel 18:32, 'I have no pleasure in the death of anyone, declares the Lord GOD; so turn and live.' The Lord Jesus also commanded, 'Go therefore and make disciples of all nations' (*Matt.* 28:19), and the willingness of God to save is expressed in the familiar words in John 3:16: 'God so loved the world, that he gave his only Son, that whoever believes in him should not perish but have eternal life.'

We should consider also the Saviour's lament over Jerusalem in Matt. 23:37, 'How often I willed to gather your children together, as a hen gathers her chicks under her wings, but you did not will.' This agrees with his words in John 5:34,40, 'I say these things that you may be saved . . . But you are not willing to come to me that you might have life.' (My translations here indicate the use of the same verb *to will*.)

This statement must then be regarded as a great encouragement to sinners to repent and turn to God, and we all ought to marvel at the extent of his love towards us in Jesus Christ (*Rom.* 5:8). The Christian church is responsible to convey these truths as the means by which God will bring men to salvation and grant them a real, personal knowledge of the truth. In this way they will prove for themselves that the trustworthy saying (*1 Tim.* 1:15) is deserving of full acceptance.

Earlier, in the doxology of 1:17, Paul emphasized that there is only *one God*, a foundation truth of the whole biblical revelation, and when the Word of the Lord was preached by him in Ephesus this fact was evidenced in the conversion of many who were delivered from false gods and associated magic arts (*Acts* 19). The repetition of this truth in verse 5 is directly linked with the revealed will of God concerning salvation since, because there is only one true God, there is and could be no other remedy for man's sinful condition than his. Therefore the Christian gospel is relevant to all men, 'For there is no distinction between Jew and Greek; the same Lord is Lord of all, bestowing his riches on all who call on him. For everyone who calls on the name of the Lord will be saved' (*Rom.* 10:12–13).

Though we are familiar with the term *mediator* it is worthwhile considering why one is necessary and what he needs to accomplish. A mediator is only necessary when there is antagonism or hostility between two parties, and so we are reminded that we were formerly alienated from God and hostile to him in our minds (*Col.* 1:21). God's wrath is actively exercised against all ungodliness and unrighteousness of men now and sinners will experience it fully in the coming day of wrath (*Rom.* 1:18; 2:5). Men are in rebellion against God and lack the ability to change their hearts or to make peace with him by their own efforts. They needed someone who was acceptable to God and willing to act on their behalf so that they might be reconciled to God. This would involve suffering the wrath of God in order that he might deliver sinners from it, and it was this that *the man Christ Jesus* accomplished (*1 Thess.* 1:10, *Rom.* 5:9.)

This mediator is identified as himself *man* for it was necessary in God's plan that his Son should partake in our common humanity, while being perfectly free from sin, holy, innocent, and unstained (*Heb.* 2:14; 7:26), in order to save us. Already Paul has written of the activity of this mediator, 'Christ Jesus came into the world to save sinners' (*1 Tim.* 1:15), and here he clarifies what it involved for him: He *gave himself as a ransom for all* (verse 6). This is how Jesus had described the purpose of his coming as the Son of Man, 'to give his life as a ransom for many' (*Matt.* 20:28). A *ransom* was the price paid to secure the release of a prisoner from his captors or a slave from his master, and our Lord's work was to rescue sinners from the power of Satan and deliver them from the punishment they deserved. The compound noun for *ransom* here (*antilutron*) necessarily involves the concept of substitution, for he gave HIMSELF in his death, and this vicarious death was on behalf of all kinds of men. While we recognize the infinite value of this ransom, it is only through faith in the Lord Jesus Christ that we receive its benefits. The truth is therefore preached to secure the repentance and faith of its hearers.

In former times this prospect was foreshadowed in the Old Testament sacrificial rituals and foretold in the Messianic promises, but now that the ransom has been paid clearer *testimony* can be borne to it, as God designed. The Lord Jesus had given his faithful eleven disciples an understanding of these matters (*Luke* 24:44–48), and sent the Holy Spirit to empower them to bear witness to him (*Acts* 1:8). So subsequently God had appointed Paul *a preacher and an apostle*, as he emphasized in his letter to the Galatians (1:1):

'Paul, an apostle — not from men nor through man, but through Jesus Christ and God the Father.' He emphasized the same thing in 1 Cor. 9:1 and 2 Cor. 12:12. Though the least of all saints, he wrote in Eph. 3:8, this grace was given to him, 'to preach to the Gentiles the unsearchable riches of Christ'. The preacher is God's herald to proclaim God's message clearly and faithfully, and this is the method by which God is pleased to save those who believe (*1 Cor.* 1:21).

It is perhaps surprising to find here this solemn double affirmation, *I am telling the truth, I am not lying*, for Timothy was surely already convinced of this through his companionship with Paul; but it does serve to impress this on all readers of this epistle, and remove any doubts about its authorship and authority.

Paul's commission, derived from Christ's own call, was to a ministry among *the Gentiles*, and on his return from his first missionary journey he and Barnabas reported 'how [God] had opened a door of faith to the Gentiles' (*Acts* 9:15, 22:21, and 14:27).

The phrase *in faith and truth* may refer to the faith that the apostle exercised in his preaching: he spoke faithfully, for this was the means by which God was pleased to save sinners, and he was truthful in the proclamation of the gospel. However, since in verse 4 he had written that God was willing for men to come to the knowledge of the truth, this expression most probably refers to the objective truth of the doctrine entrusted to him.

7

Directions for Congregational Worship

I desire then that in every place the men should pray, lifting holy hands, without anger or quarrelling; ⁹ likewise also that women should adorn themselves in respectable apparel, with modesty and self-control, not with braided hair and gold or pearls or costly attire, ¹⁰ but with what is proper for women who profess godliness—with good works (1 Tim. 2:8–10).

These verses clearly relate to the occasions when Christians meet together for worship and the words suggest that the church at Ephesus comprised several congregations that gathered in different locations. They may have continued to use the hall of Tyrannus (*Acts* 19:9), but probably met in some of the members' houses as seems to have been normal in those early years. This is mentioned in Philemon 2, 'The church in your house', and Colossians 4:15, 'Nympha and the church in her house'.

Paul begins by commanding that men should offer public prayer in congregational worship, for though we have the verb *desire* it does express the deliberate exercise of volition, and so must be recognized as the communication of a command under the authority of the Lord Jesus Christ. This is implied by the linking word *then*. It is part of Paul's instructions to Timothy in his responsibility of guiding the conduct of the church, for in this realm everything should be done decently and in the God-given order (*1 Cor.* 14:40).

The following brief description of the manner of prayer makes reference both to posture and to the disposition of one's heart and mind. We have an example of the *lifting up of hands* in 1 Kings 8:22 when Solomon 'stood in the presence of all the assembly of

Israel and spread out his hands toward heaven', and in the command in Psalm 134:2, 'Lift up your hands to the holy place and bless the LORD!' Moses also is recorded as triumphing in prayer for the Israelite victory over the Amalekites when he continued to lift up his hands in prayer (*Exod.* 17:11–12).

At the practical level it is obviously helpful for the congregation if the man who leads in public prayer does stand, as it will assist all present to hear and say the 'Amen' with understanding and true devotion.

The lifting up of hands is also a suitable expression of our pleading with God and, when they are open, of the expectation to receive from him what we ask for, as the Lord Jesus taught in Mark 11:24, 'Whatever you ask in prayer, believe that you have received it, and it will be yours.'

It is however plain in the Scriptures that standing is not the only acceptable posture, for David sat before the LORD when he prayed (*2 Sam.* 7:18), and it seems that Daniel's regular practice was to kneel in prayer (*Dan.* 6:10), while Paul refers to his own prayer in Ephesians 3:14, 'I bow my knees before the Father.' Jesus himself in the Garden of Gethsemane both knelt down (*Luke* 22:41), and fell on his face (*Matt.* 26:39), when he engaged in most earnest prayer, as Moses had done when pleading for Israel (*Deut.* 9:25). When awed by a revelation of God's majestic glory men frequently prostrated themselves before him with their faces to the ground (*2 Chron.* 7:3, *Ezek.* 1:28; 3:22, *Rev.* 11:16).

The position of the hands is plainly less important than the disposition of the heart, for holiness and genuine devotion originate there and find their expression in hands that are not involved in sinful practices. Those who desire to stand in God's holy place should have clean hands and a pure heart (*Psa.* 24:4), and we are exhorted in James 4:8, 'Draw near to God, and he will draw near to you. Cleanse your hands, you sinners, and purify your hearts, you double-minded.' Prayers should be made *without anger*, probably here in the sense of an agitated mind that often gives vent to the desire for vengeance, for not all anger is sinful. However Christians should be concerned that those who have sinned against them should be forgiven, as the Lord Jesus taught in Matt. 6:14–15, and repeated in Mark. 11:25.

The word *dialogismois* (reasonings) in verse 8 may mean 'doubting' (AV, NKJV). When we pray we should not entertain doubts or inward questionings about God's willingness to hear and answer but rather ask in faith (*James* 1:6–7), for those who ask with doubting must not suppose they will receive anything from the Lord. But there is a wider meaning of the word that includes *quarrelling* and disputing, and its link with wrath here may warrant that sense, so that the application will be as Chrysostom suggested, 'Our minds should be calm and free from all uneasy feelings towards God and towards men.' 'We ought to pray with a peaceful conscience and assured confidence' (Calvin).

Paul proceeds in the same manner to give directions to women, but he does not assign to them any distinctive role or activity in congregational worship, though he expects that, like most men, they will participate communally in the praise of God and in the prayers made to God, besides listening to God as his Word is read and preached.

As members of the church they are required to *adorn themselves* with the qualities and actions that are proper for those who profess godliness. The word translated *apparel* includes the demeanour that is outwardly exhibited in dressing modestly, and this is explained more clearly by the following nouns. *Modesty*, translated 'decency' in the NIV and 'shamefacedness' in the AV, denotes a genuine respect for what is truly honourable and will not offend others, and for the Christian that primarily means a concern for God's approval.

Self-control is well defined by Ellicott as, 'the well balanced state of mind resulting from habitual self-restraint'. It is important to concentrate on these distinctive virtues that should characterize Christian women because God is concerned mainly with what is in their heads and hearts, rather than with their outward appearance, though what they are inwardly should be demonstrated in how they dress.

This is explained as the apostle continues his teaching about a woman's adornment by describing a contrasting and inappropriate style of dressing that fails to express the distinctive inner Christian disposition. All must be careful when they gather for congregational worship to prepare themselves inwardly because they desire to come into the presence of God in an acceptable manner, and avoid any distraction caused by what they or others wear. The apostle Peter was also constrained by the Lord to guide women in this matter, 'Do not let your adorning be external—the braiding of hair, the wearing of gold, or the putting on of clothing—but let your adorning be the hidden person of the heart, with the imperishable beauty of a gentle and quiet spirit, which in God's sight is very precious' (*1 Pet.* 3:3–4). Braiding and plaiting of the hair could be very time-consuming as well as expensive, like the elaborate coiffures of modern times. Gold and pearls and costly garments were the prerogatives of the rich and the ostentatious display of wealth is hardly fitting for those who seek to worship God in humility of spirit. 'Showy clothes ill befit broken and contrite hearts, the hearts which God welcomes at the service of the Word and Sacraments' (E. K. Simpson).

This is also closely linked to the Christian view of wealth, namely that God has entrusted it to some of his children, not for selfish ends but for the good of others, so that they should abound rather in the grace of giving as taught in 2 Corinthians, chapters 8 and 9, and exemplified in our Lord Jesus Christ (*2 Cor.* 8:9). Clearly this is relevant here because Paul specifically mentions *good works*. These will cause those who observe them to glorify God, as is commanded by the Lord (*Matt.* 5:16); and we all are taught to do good (*1 Tim.* 6:18), especially to those who are of the household of faith (*Gal.* 6:10).

8

The Place of Women in the Church

Let a woman learn quietly with all submissiveness. [12] *I do not permit a woman to teach or to exercise authority over a man; rather, she is to remain quiet.* [13] *For Adam was formed first, then Eve;* [14] *and Adam was not deceived, but the woman was deceived and became a transgressor.* [15] *Yet she will be saved through childbearing—if they continue in faith and love and holiness, with self-control* (1 Tim. 2:11–15).

This section has aroused much discussion, especially in recent years, because of the rise of the feminist movement and its impact on the Christian church, so we must be careful to discover and define accurately what it is that is actually taught by the apostle Paul.

Firstly, we observe that it is expected that women will learn to make good use of the scriptural instruction provided within the church and by their own reading of God's Word, with prayerful meditation. The intellectual abilities with which God has endowed a woman must not be restricted but be fully employed, and particularly she must take the Saviour's yoke upon her and learn of him (*Matt.* 11:29).

She must however *learn quietly*, without inner turmoil or exasperation at being forbidden to speak in the church meetings, and also, together with all other Christians, should humbly submit to the truths that are taught. This command has a parallel, and further comment, in 1 Corinthians 14:34–35, 'The women should keep silent in the churches. For they are not permitted to speak, but should be in submission, as the Law also says. If there is anything they desire to learn, let them ask their husbands at home. For it is shameful for a woman to speak in church.' 'Church' here is to be understood as the assembled congregation, not the building where it meets. Women must submit to this apostolic command to remain silent by not intruding into the realm of teaching in the church, for they have been excluded by God from this special responsibility and activity. In his perfect wisdom and supreme authority God has entrusted it to some men whom he has chosen to serve him in the church, the elders whose qualifications are revealed in 1 Timothy 3:1–7. It should be recognized that, since most men are also barred from the teaching office in the church, this is not really a matter of sexual discrimination but only one of divine order that includes everyone.

This limitation of a woman's activity in the life of the congregation is connected with another principle that within the church she must not *exercise authority over a man*. It is important to recognize that this restriction on a woman's teaching applies only to the church meetings for worship, for she shares the task with men of bearing witness to the Lord Jesus. This can be deduced from Romans 16, where Paul commends many women for their activities that benefited the life of their churches; Phoebe is described as 'a servant of the church at Cenchreae', verse 1; Mary 'worked hard for you', verse 6; and Persis 'worked hard in the Lord', verse 12. In Philippians 4:2–3 he speaks of women 'who have laboured side by side with me in the gospel'; and Priscilla shared with her husband Aquila in explaining to Apollos 'the way of God more accurately' (*Acts* 18:26).

In Titus 2:3–4 we are taught that older women are to 'teach what is good, and so train the young women to love their husbands and children.'

Later in 1 Timothy (*1 Tim.* 5:10), it is indicated that Christian women can render valuable service to the life of a congregation by undertaking practical duties like showing hospitality and caring for the afflicted. There are many spheres of Christian service that are open to women, so that no-one who truly wants to serve the Lord in ways he approves should feel excluded from opportunities to do so. The Lord Jesus Christ has chosen to rule his church by selected men as elders. Their task as teachers necessarily implies the exercise of authority, and he has appointed men to represent his headship in teaching.

The exclusion of women from the teaching office is a particular outworking of their subordinate role in the man-woman relationship that is taught in the Old Testament and explained here. This was implicit in the order of creation as revealed in Genesis 2:7, 'The LORD God formed the man of dust from the ground and breathed into his nostrils the breath of life, and the man became a living creature.' Then later he said, 'It is not good that the man should be alone; I will make him a helper fit for him'; and he did so by taking a rib from Adam and making it into a woman (verses 18, 22).

The truth drawn from this account is that the woman was made out of a man for the sake of the man, to be his companion and not his ruler, whereas man, who is the image and glory of God, was constituted the head of the woman (*1 Cor.* 11:3, 7–9). There is no suggestion that the female Christian is in any way inferior to the male as a believer for they both equally enjoy all the blessings of salvation as the children of God. This is clearly taught in Galatians 3:28: 'There is neither Jew nor Greek, there is neither slave nor free, there is neither male nor female, for you are all one in Christ Jesus.' Paul does not here teach that these racial and social distinctions are abolished, for they obviously remain; so clearly does that based on sexual difference. What is emphasized rather is that, in their relationship with the Lord Jesus, Christian men and Christian women are equal as God's children.

A second reason for the distinctive roles of men and women in Christ's church is the fact that it was Eve who was initially totally deceived by Satan and then herself took of the fruit of the tree of knowledge of good and evil and gave some to Adam who also ate (*Gen.* 3:1–6). Eve in this act subverted the divine order by leading, and among the consequences was subjection to the rule of her husband, a rule that would be less agreeable than before they sinned (*Gen.* 3:16).

Since they are both sinful, the rule of men may become improperly domineering and women may resent even the legitimate exercise of that rule, and both need to recognize their own weaknesses and failures in the relationship and seek God's enabling to change for the better. Women are viewed as the daughters of Eve so that like her she must be subject to her husband in the marriage relationship (*Eph.* 5:22, *Col.* 3:18, *1 Pet.* 3:1), as well as to the men Christ has appointed to rule in his church.

The closing verse (verse 15) is one of the most notoriously difficult texts in Paul's letters, but since it was written for our benefit we must seek its meaning and relevance to us. We begin by tracing the connection of thought with the words of the Lord God to Eve in Genesis 3:16, 'I will surely multiply your pain in childbearing; in pain you shall bring forth children.' The significance of this divine sentence is well taught by E. J. Young: 'She will be able to propagate the race, so God has just promised, but her life will be one in which this very function of reproduction will remind her of her fall and disobedience' (*Genesis 3*, Banner of Truth, 1966, p. 123). However these pains are not an unmitigated sorrow for a mother, according to the Lord Jesus, who said, 'When a woman . . . has delivered the baby, she no longer remembers the anguish, for joy that a human being has been born into the world' (*John* 16:21). Mothers generally lovingly care for their children and joyfully nourish them, finding pleasure in that relationship and in their involvement in the early development of their children, and valuing this as a privilege granted to them.

Childbearing is also to be acknowledged as obedience to the divine command to be fruitful and multiply (*Gen.* 1:28), and within the family Christian mothers share with fathers the responsibility to bring up children in the discipline and instruction of the Lord (*Eph.* 6:4). We cannot begin to estimate the contribution that the faithful discharge of motherhood has made to the welfare and growth of the Christian church, and of course Timothy himself had benefited from the instruction of his believing mother and grandmother in the truths of the Scriptures (*2 Tim.* 1:5, 3:15). The beneficial influence of Augustine's mother, Monica, on him during his early wayward years, through her continued earnest prayer for him, together with her witness to him by scripture truth and by her Christian character, is also a great example in the history of the Christian church of the value and importance of Christian motherhood.

The major difficulty posed by this verse is to resolve what is meant by, 'She will be saved through childbearing—if they continue in faith and love and holiness, with self-control.' Since it is evident that some Christian women are not preserved alive in giving birth to their children, this cannot be a blanket statement about physical safety; and equally it is clear that childbearing cannot bring or contribute to spiritual salvation.

Some would interpret the reference to childbearing in the light of the distinct contribution that this unique feminine privilege allows a woman to make to family and to church life. These interpreters then go on to say that, when she is faithful in this realm, she makes progress in salvation. However, the question would then arise, Are women who cannot or do not bear children disadvantaged? It would also seem a rather complicated, not to say obscure, way of teaching this truth.

Another explanation, and one that I prefer, is found by noting that the apostle actually wrote of '*the* childbearing'. When this is related to the promise in Genesis 3:15 concerning the offspring of the woman who would crush the serpent's head, we find a prophetic reference to the childbearing of Mary, the mother of the Lord Jesus. As most blessed among women (*Luke* 1:42), Mary was chosen by God to conceive a child by the agency of the Holy Spirit who would be this unique promised seed. Through her giving birth to the Lord Jesus Christ, the Son of God incarnate, this promise was fulfilled.

We may then understand that Paul teaches here that 'the childbearing' was that unique event by which the Saviour, born of the virgin Mary, came as the one Mediator between God and man (verse 5). This was the way in which he 'came into the world to save sinners' (*1 Tim.* 1:15). Eve's name, which means 'the mother of all living' (*Gen.* 3:20), can also be cited as a warrant for accepting this explanation of 'the childbearing'. Salvation was ultimately to come though her promised offspring.

All women—we must note the change in verse 15 to the plural 'they'—whether or not they are mothers, are encouraged to continue in their exercise of faith, believing the divine promises and trusting the Saviour, however that faith may be tested. They must recall the command of 1 Timothy 1:5 and abound in love. This is also commended in 1 John 5:3: 'This is the love of God, that we keep his commandments. And his commandments are not burdensome.' This is the way in which they will become more holy, for sanctification is progressive, and their increasing holiness will include *self-control*, that well-balanced state of mind that will lead them humbly and gladly to honour God by obedience to his commands. The apostle expects that Christian women, concerned to do the will of God, will respond positively to all his teaching, to please their Lord and Saviour who is its real Author.

9

The Divinely-Imposed
Qualifications for Church Elders

*The saying is trustworthy: If anyone aspires to the office of over-
seer, he desires a noble task. ² Therefore an overseer must be above
reproach, the husband of one wife, sober-minded, self-controlled,
respectable, hospitable, able to teach, ³ not a drunkard, not violent but
gentle, not quarrelsome, not a lover of money. ⁴ He must manage his
own household well, with all dignity keeping his children submissive,
⁵ for if someone does not know how to manage his own household, how
will he care for God's church? ⁶ He must not be a recent convert, or
he may become puffed up with conceit and fall into the condemnation
of the devil. ⁷ Moreover, he must be well thought of by outsiders, so
that he may not fall into disgrace, into a snare of the devil* (1 Tim.
3:1–7).

We have already noted that the church of the Lord Jesus
Christ must be founded and built up on the healthy doctrine of the apostles, and that it was the responsibility of Timothy
to ensure that this was done in Ephesus. He was to do so holding
firmly to the faith with a good conscience and was charged firstly
to direct the church in the realm of her worship and, in particular,
her prayer life. This led Paul to distinguish the roles of men and
women in the congregation. He now proceeds to give instructions
about the organized life of the church and begins in this section
to introduce the first of the church officers who were to serve the
Lord within her.

The excellence of their work is emphasized by the introduction,
'The saying is trustworthy.' This indicates that Christians widely
acknowledged that such a task when rightly discharged was a valu-

able part of Christ's provision for the welfare of his church. The title of this office is the Greek word *episkopos*. It is translated in the AV and NKJV as 'bishop', though in Acts 20:28 these versions use 'overseer'. The noun 'bishop' apparently came into use through the Old English *biscop*, itself derived from this Greek noun.

Since the meaning of the term 'bishop' is now affected by its use in various ecclesiastical systems, it is probably better to follow the example of the NIV and ESV and use the term 'overseer', which shows something of the nature of the work: the *episkopos* was to supervise or superintend the congregation's life. From the LXX we learn that God himself exercised this oversight on behalf of his chosen people (*Exod.* 3:16), and he appointed men to look after their welfare as a shepherd cares for his sheep (*Jer.* 23:2). Because they failed in this task he then promised in Ezekiel 34:11 to shepherd them himself, and the Lord Jesus exercises this ministry as 'the good shepherd' (*John* 10:11). He is called in 1 Peter 2:25, 'the Shepherd and Overseer (*episkopos*) of your souls'.

That Christ as the Head of the church has appointed men to discharge this task of caring oversight among his people is shown in Acts 1:20, where Peter quotes Psalm 109:8, and applies it to the office (Greek, *episkope*) that Matthias was to exercise in the place of Judas as his successor among the apostles. This term then has a relevant Old Testament background, but it was also a title used among the Greeks of a person who presided over a religious society or who was commissioned by superiors to oversee the life of a community.

There is another equivalent term used of the overseer, namely 'elder'. Besides denoting an older person, this was used in secular contemporary writings as a mark of the dignity possessed by those holding civic and religious offices, rather like the English term 'alderman'. Among God's chosen nation in Old Testament times, the title 'elder' described the heads of tribal divisions and chief officers of cities, but we may particularly note the foundational reference in Numbers 11:17,25. There it is recorded that God granted seventy elders of Israel a special gift of the Holy Spirit to bear the burden with Moses in ruling and guiding the people. We should not therefore be surprised to find it also used to describe those with spiritual responsibility in the church, and we note the presence of elders in the Jerusalem church (*Acts* 15:2, 4, etc.). When Paul and Barnabas concluded the first missionary journey they did not take the shortest route back to Palestine but returned to the cities visited with the gospel and ordained elders in every church (*Acts* 14:23), indicating the importance of this office. This had obviously been done at Ephesus for Paul called the elders from there to meet him at Miletus (*Acts* 20:17), and in his address to them the task of an elder is identified with that of an overseer, as is confirmed elsewhere in the New Testament. Titus was to appoint elders in every city in Crete, and they are later called overseers (*Titus* 1:5,7). The elders addressed in 1 Peter 5:1–2 are expected to 'shepherd the flock of God . . . exercising oversight'. The mention of these responsibilities recalls Ephesians 4:11–12 in which we are taught that the Lord Jesus Christ gave some to be pastors and teachers for the edifying of the body of Christ.

Since many elders and bishops in the professing church through the centuries have completely failed to meet these scriptural standards and fulfil the duties God requires, it is vital that Christians today should carefully consider and apply the guidance provided in these pastoral letters regarding the choice of elders, as, by divine authority, the apostle sets out the qualifications for overseers or elders in verses 2–7, and also in Titus 1:5–9.

Though it would be improper for any person to take the office on himself, it is quite acceptable that he should *aspire* to serve the Lord and his church in this good work (verse 1). However, he must submit himself to the judgment of others concerning his suitability. This includes elements of character and behaviour, so that he is *above reproach*, blameless so far as others observe his relationships and the way he lives. It is important as we consider the several requirements to note that perfection is not among them! But of course elders, as all Christians, should press forward to it (*Phil.* 3:12–14). The list is quite diverse, and our study in the following sections will have to be fairly detailed.

1. *The husband of one wife.* This need not be interpreted as an absolute requirement for elders to be married, but if the candidate for oversight is married, then he must have only one wife and so exemplify and be able to teach the scriptural Christian view of

marriage. Though this clearly excludes polygamists, it serves also as a warning that elders must abstain from all sexual activities that breach the seventh commandment (1:10), and those guilty should be disciplined by removal from office. However, it does not seem to prohibit a widowed elder from marrying a second wife.

2. The next three characteristics (*sober-minded, self-controlled, respectable*) are related to a man's self-discipline. He is to be temperate, morally alert, and circumspect in his conduct, moderate in his use of all things, and not under the power of distracting or addictive influences. He should rather exercise *self-control*. This quality was commended in 2:9,15. It means that he will be discreet in what he says and does. His good behaviour will make him *respectable*, though, in addition to outward conduct, this term refers to the well-ordering of one's inner life, revealed in a balanced conduct which commends the Christian faith as worthy of honour.

3. To be *hospitable* literally means showing friendship to strangers, and elders ought to take the lead in this responsibility which is commended to all Christians in Romans 12:13 (where it is linked with contributing to the needs of the saints) and in 1 Peter 4:9.

Overseers should gladly give both time and energy as an expression of Christian love to help fellow-believers (*Heb.* 13:1–2). Such hospitality should, when appropriate, extend to the provision of food and shelter, especially to those who are suffering persecution or are on journeys in the service of the Lord, a benefit that Paul himself had frequently enjoyed.

4. A major part of the work of the overseer in the Christian church involved gaining a good understanding of Scripture truth in order to communicate and apply it to others, so that those who aspired to this office needed to reveal an aptitude to *teach*. This cannot mean that teachers of any subject are thereby necessarily suitable, but that overseers should be *able to teach* what the Word of God means, so that those who hear may understand and respond aright. We have a good example of this in Nehemiah 8:8: 'They read from the book, from the Law of God, clearly, and they gave the meaning, so that the people understood the reading.' Faithful

exposition of the Scripture can only be built upon careful exegesis of the truth as originally communicated by God, in relation to other relevant passages. It requires that prospective overseers have a clear understanding of the basic truths of the Christian faith, and a biblical theology, so that they 'hold firm to the trustworthy word as taught' and can encourage others and 'give instruction in sound [or healthy] doctrine' (*Titus* 1:9). Later Timothy was commanded to entrust what he had heard from Paul in the presence of many witnesses to faithful men who would be able to teach others also (*2 Tim.* 2:2).

5. The prospective overseer must not be *addicted to wine* (verse 3). The phrase is less specific than the noun *drunkard*, but carries a warning against the effects of the consequent befuddled state of mind that will lead to unseemly language and even violent acts. This does not mean that elders must totally abstain from wine and other potentially intoxicating drink, for the Lord Jesus turned water into wine (*John* 2:9), and used wine in the institution of the Lord's Supper (*Matt.* 26:29). Paul actually commended it to Timothy: 'Use a little wine for the sake of your stomach and your frequent ailments' (5:23). However, voluntary abstinence is commendable, especially when it is designed to help those who have a 'drink problem', and in the presence of those who would be caused to stumble (*Rom.* 14:15,21). To do otherwise could prove to be a failure to walk in love.

6. Other qualities required are expressed negatively and begin with *not violent*, for the man who is belligerent and ready to bully others with force or threats is unfitted to the shepherding of Christ's flock. One criticism that the LORD made of Israel's shepherds was that they ruled his sheep with force and harshness (*Ezek.* 34:4), and sadly within the Christian church such conduct is not unknown, though contrary to the example and teaching of her Lord and Saviour. The positive virtue in contrast with this wrong behaviour is that of the *gentleness* which was characteristic of the Lord himself: 'the meekness and gentleness of Christ' (*2 Cor.* 10:1), and includes what has been called 'sweet reasonableness', a graciousness of attitude towards others. This virtue is included in the wisdom that

is from above, mentioned in James 3:17, where it is linked with a willingness to yield in the interests of an honourable peace, and is not quarrelsome, nor easily provoked. In 2 Timothy 2:24–25 we have further guidance: 'And the Lord's servant must not be quarrelsome but kind to everyone, able to teach, patiently enduring evil, correcting his opponents with gentleness.'

7. The last potential fault lies in one's attitude to wealth. The overseer must *not* be *a lover of money*. Our Lord criticized the Pharisees for their love of money (*Luke* 16:14–15), when they derided his teaching that 'You cannot serve God and mammon' (*Luke* 16:13). This indicates that the fault can be concealed from others by an outward show of righteousness. All Christians are urged, 'Keep your life free from love of money, and be content with what you have', with the sufficient reason that, 'he has said, "I will never leave you nor forsake you"' (*Heb.* 13:5). The betrayal of the Lord Jesus for thirty pieces of silver by his disciple Judas Iscariot was the culmination of his love of money, previously shown in stealing from the money bag (*John* 12:6). This illustrates the danger most forcefully.

It is appropriate here to pause and to realize that the descriptions given are not simply designed as the means by which we are to observe characteristics of those who desire to be overseers, but are also a mirror by which we should examine ourselves. Since an overseer should be an example to the flock (*1 Tim.* 4:12, *1 Pet.* 5:3), so the members of the flock ought to imitate him as he imitates Christ (*1 Cor.* 11:1). In 6:6–10, 17–19, the apostle returns to the topic of the Christian attitude to money, and we will defer further comment until we consider those passages.

8. The apostle turns next in verses 4 and 5 to the need for the overseer to *manage* (or preside over) *his own household well* in the role of husband and father in the manner appointed by God (*Eph.* 5:25, 6:4; *Col.* 3:19, 21; and *1 Pet.* 3:7). This would include these observable elements: he will love his wife as Christ loved the church, and bring his children up in the discipline and instruction of the Lord; there should be no selfish tyranny but a focus on the welfare of his whole family, primarily in the spiritual realm to please the

Lord; and the children should be kept subject to scriptural discipline with all dignity or proper respect. He will try to educate them in the sound doctrine of godliness and in the fear of the Lord, both encouraging them to grow in grace and self-control, and also restraining them from insubordination to lawful authority. There is a solemn warning to reinforce this command in 1 Samuel 3:13, where the LORD informs Samuel that he will judge Eli's family because Eli did not restrain his sons from their vile conduct. Failure in the governing of his household would indicate that the man desiring to be an elder was not competent to take care of the church of God.

We note the significant change of the verb from *manage* to one that indicates the attentive *care* illustrated in the kind and compassionate action of the Good Samaritan in meeting the needs of the man robbed and wounded by thieves (*Luke* 10:34–35). The overseer/elder must have a like loving care for the church in which God has appointed him, a caring concern that involves nourishing its members on the truths of God's Word, comforting the fainthearted, and upholding the weak (*1 Thess.* 5:14).

9. The candidate for office should *not* be *a recent convert*, that is, still a babe in Christ, but one who has become spiritually mature, and who by constant practice has had his powers of discernment trained (*Heb.* 5:14), approving what is excellent (*Phil.* 1:10). It is necessary that he be prepared over a period of time by the submission of his mind to the truths of God's Word and by incorporating these truths in his lifestyle, though there is a diversity of methods in what is termed 'Ministerial Training'. Those most sincerely concerned to honour the Lord as overseers in his church, that is, to serve him as pastors and teachers, will take on this work with the greatest seriousness and be unwilling to thrust themselves forward presumptuously. The danger of the novice is that his inexperience will lead to pride, so that he is 'blinded or bewildered with self-conceit', as Alford describes this condition. This would expose him to the same condemnation that God visited on the devil. Though from conversion a Christian should be a good witness to the Lord Jesus, he needs to grow up in Christ, becoming mature in his thinking, before intruding into the ministry of Christ's church.

10. The last consideration is that a man should be *well thought of by outsiders*. Presumably this means non-Christians who know him well, and have discerned the real nature and quality of his life. Though they are ignorant of the inner transforming power of Christ, they will recognize whether what the man says and does (or does not say and do) accords with what they know of the faith that he professes.

A Christian may maintain an acceptable standard of conduct among fellow believers but accommodate himself to the lifestyle of the unconverted when in their company. When he behaves contrary to the teaching of Scripture he brings reproach on himself and falls into a trap set by the devil. None can dare to forget that there is a cunning enemy, the devil, who maliciously seeks to discredit the Christian faith by any means he can, and all Christians must resist him by being steadfast in the faith and consistent in their practice. It is profitable to consider what our neighbours or work colleagues think of us: how obvious is it to them that we are genuine Christians?

The Lord's Requirements for Deacons

Deacons likewise must be dignified, not double-tongued, not addicted to much wine, not greedy for dishonest gain. ⁹ They must hold the mystery of the faith with a clear conscience. ¹⁰ And let them also be tested first; then let them serve as deacons if they prove themselves blameless. ¹¹ Their wives likewise must be dignified, not slanderers, but sober-minded, faithful in all things. ¹² Let deacons each be the husband of one wife, managing their children and their own households well. ¹³ For those who serve well as deacons gain a good standing for themselves and also great confidence in the faith that is in Christ Jesus (1 Tim. 3:8–13).

This section (verses 8–13) is concerned to provide guidance in the selection of deacons by stating the appropriate qualifications, and is thus parallel with that devoted to elders (verses 1–7). It is therefore immediately apparent that this is a different office in the church from that of eldership, and this distinction is plain in Philippians 1:1 where Paul addresses *the overseers and deacons*.

The precise nature of the deacons' work is not here identified and has been disputed for centuries, but we must cull from the Scriptures what information we can to guide us. The first clue lies in the term 'deacon' itself. It is virtually a transliteration of the Greek word (*diakonos*) whose basic meaning is servant. He is therefore one who serves Christ in the life of his church. Clearly many others serve, so that often both the servant and his service are unrelated to this office. The Lord Jesus himself came to serve and the whole of his public ministry was in service to God and men, culminating in his giving his life a ransom for many (*Mark* 10:45).

Early in the history of the church a form of practical service (Greek, *diakonia*) was established to minister to the needs of the poor, especially of widows. This was initially under the direction of the apostles at Jerusalem (*Acts* 4:35 and 6:1–2). When the number of disciples there multiplied, the twelve said, 'It is not right that we should give up preaching the word of God to serve tables' (*Acts* 6:2), and they guided the Christians to choose seven men whom they would appoint to the duty of serving tables. Though the term 'deacon' is not applied to the seven, it is plain that they were appointed to practical service in distributing the church's alms, and often this apostolically-directed event is regarded as the institution of the office.

This service was under the supervision firstly of the apostles, and later of the elders, as indicated in Acts 11:30, where the relief given by Christians at Antioch as service to the brethren in Jerusalem was sent to the elders. John Calvin taught that the Scripture especially gives the name of deacons 'to those whom the Church appoints to dispense alms, and take care of the poor' (*Institutes*, Book IV, ch.3, sect. 9). In the fulfilment of their duty they were obviously assistants of the elders or overseers, but the absence of a requirement that they be 'able to teach' would seem to imply that their assistance did not extend into the realm of teaching God's Word.

Since there is some overlap with the qualifications for the overseer it seems wise to concentrate on those directly related to deacons. We immediately observe that they lie in the domain of Christian morality and adherence to Christian doctrines.

The opening description (verse 8) is positive and stands emphatically before the others. Deacons *must be dignified*. The older word is venerable, meaning worthy of respect, so that other Christians admire their character and their comely demeanour. This is in accord with the demands of Peter concerning those who would serve in Acts 6:3, for they were to be 'men of good repute, full of the Spirit and of wisdom'.

There follow three defects that would prevent a man from being admitted into the deacon's office. He must *not* be *double-tongued;* that is, he must be discreet in all his conversation, not deceitful in his words, and not given to sharing gossip or betraying confidences. This fault is exposed in the LXX version of Proverbs 11:13: 'A double-tongued man discloses the secret counsels of an assembly', though the translation of the Hebrew in the ESV is, 'Whoever goes about slandering reveals secrets.' In his service, a deacon would be aware of private personal problems and situations that it would be improper for him to make public.

Like the overseer he must *not* be *addicted to much wine,* but careful if he drinks that it does not impair his service or ruin his character.

Because he handles money for the benefit of others, the deacon must not himself be *greedy for dishonest gain.* The same warning is given with regard to elders in Titus 1:7 and indicates that any such dishonourable action is shameful, whether it involves dishonesty in the distribution of money or abuse of it for personal profit. We should note that financial acumen is not required, only integrity!

In verse 9 we are directed to spiritual qualifications. Deacons must have an intelligent and believing grasp of Christian doctrine and preserve a good conscience. By *the mystery of the faith* Paul refers to the fundamental truths of the Christian message that have been revealed by God, 'the sum of Christian doctrine' (Calvin). The term *mystery* denotes something that cannot be discovered by human intelligence but can only be made known by God, and he was pleased to reveal this mystery of faith through his inspired chosen servants, by whom it has been written down in the God-breathed holy Scriptures.

In Ephesians 3:3–4 Paul had written of the mystery of Christ that was made known to him by revelation. He wrote briefly of this so that the readers could perceive his insight into the mystery of Christ. The person of the Lord Jesus Christ and his work as the Saviour are the central elements of the mystery and Paul returns to the consideration of them in verse 16 of this chapter. Deacons need a good understanding of the Christian faith in their work so that, besides assisting the needy in material ways, they can also share relevant truths to comfort or encourage them. To discharge their God-given service aright they must also maintain *a clear conscience,* so that their service is pleasing to God as well as really beneficial to fellow-Christians. This is the third time in 1 Timothy that Paul has taught the importance of an enlightened and cleansed conscience and its link with the exercise of faith. Every Christian must be concerned to possess such a conscience.

Before deacons enter into the exercise of their office they are to be *tested* (verse 10) in the light of these qualifications and receive the approval of the church. We assume that the congregation will have been able to observe and assess the quality of their lives and the testimony they bear to the Lord Jesus Christ and so make judgements accordingly without improper bias or favouritism. The nature of the test is not explained though it may include giving them the opportunity to serve so that an assessment may be made about their suitability by those who have personal experience of their service.

There is some difficulty in establishing how we should understand the reference to *their wives* in verse 11. Though this is a possible translation, the reference could be more generally to women who contribute in practical ways to the welfare of the congregation. In favour of the understanding, *deacons' wives,* is the fact that the words belong within a brief section concerned with the office and work of deacons. Since the deacons' service extended to widows we can appreciate that it would often be advisable if their wives assisted and accompanied them. Certainly in some cultures today that would be considered not only appropriate but necessary. Though the wife of an overseer should have the same spiritual and moral qualifications, the fact she could not share in her husband's ruling and teaching office meant that there was no need to mention her in this way.

Another view is that this refers to women who actually shared in the work of deacons as established church officers, and were called deaconesses. However, since Paul could have used the equivalent feminine term and did not do so, this view does not seem to be correct. It would be strange if a deaconess was exempt from the other qualifications that deacons had to meet. Furthermore, if there were deaconesses, the rest of the New Testament is strangely silent about them and their work. Even in 1 Timothy 5 where there is a lengthy passage concerning the enrolment of true widows, there is no mention of deaconesses, though that was a sphere in which they would most likely be of help. In Romans 16:1–2, where Phoebe is commended for her practical assistance to Paul and others, she is not given the title 'deaconess' but only described as 'a servant of the church at Cenchreae'.

[57]

A possible third interpretation is that this verse is designed to remind any woman who wants to give assistance in the life of the congregation, but without any official status, that she must meet the standards of Christian life that are here spelled out. This would accord with the undoubted fact that there were many such women who gave devoted service to other believers, like those whose names are found in Romans 16, and Lydia who housed Paul and Silas at Philippi. We appreciate that their experience and expertise in giving hospitality would always be valued by other Christians and should surely be recognized as a realm in which they could serve the Lord. Certainly this is commended in 5:10 as valuable evidence in assessing the character of widows who deserved honour. We have previously noted in our comment on 2:12 that older Christian women are encouraged in Titus 2:3–4 to train younger ones in the realm of family life.

The demeanour of such women should warrant the respect that was appropriate for any one who serves the Lord, and they are also charged not to be *slanderers*. The noun used here is the same as that used in verses 6–7 of this chapter and elsewhere as a description of the devil (*diabolos*). What they must carefully avoid is making false accusations against other Christians. This would be to behave like the devil, who is the father of lies, as the Lord Jesus taught in John 8:44. The older women addressed in Titus 2:3 were also solemnly warned against this misuse of their tongues, which would be hurtful for those wrongly accused and damage the fellowship and mutual trust among the members of the congregation. Like elders (verse 2) they are to be *sober-minded*, keeping their minds clear and vigilant, to which they should add the further quality of being *faithful in all things*. They are to be trustworthy as persons and reliable in any service they render to the congregation, and especially they should loyally fulfil their responsibilities within their families.

After this short digression the apostle returns to his teaching about deacons and adds another requirement for office that lies in the realm of the family. If the previous verse does refer to *their wives*, such an addition is not inappropriate since it is insisted that the deacon be *the husband of* only *one wife* and *manage his own household*, including his *children, well,* just as was expected of the overseer or elder (verse 2).

This section concludes with an encouragement for *those who serve well*. This could be a general conclusion relating to both elders and deacons, since in the Greek text we have only the verb *to serve*, to which many versions have added *as deacons*. Those who do serve excellently obtain for themselves *a good standing* within the congregation that will further enable them to fulfil their service with the respect and confidence of the members. It is certainly a great blessing and advantage to the church when its officers discharge their responsibilities in the manner of God's appointment. It would be wrong however to restrict it to human approbation, for faithful service that honours God is also honoured by God (*1 Sam.* 2:30), often in the realm of greater usefulness.

There is no warrant here for the suggestion that Paul teaches that the deacon by serving well in that office can secure his promotion to become an overseer. This was a much later interpretation and application of the verse and seems to have emerged in the third century of the church, with no clear evidence of it previously. It is still found in the Anglican Communion, for there those who exercise the ministry of the Word of God begin to serve as deacons. This is not to deny that, if men did commend themselves to the church as deacons, then they could be considered for the work of the overseer; but they would need to meet the extra qualifications mentioned above. We find in Acts that two who first served as deacons, Stephen and Philip, later became preachers of the gospel, but there is no hint that this was to become a precedent, and in fact they are not referred to as overseers or elders.

This *good standing* is accompanied by *great confidence* (or much boldness) *in the faith*, as the man both approaches God in prayer (*Heb.* 4:16), and also serves God within the church. This confidence is in the realm of faith in Christ and would seem to embrace both his personal trust in Christ and his commitment to the Christian faith.

It is probably right to consider that this boldness may be related to that awesome day when all God's servants must give account of their stewardship. Then the Lord will say to some, 'Well done good and faithful servant' (*Matt.* 25:21). Certainly this is apparent in the words of the apostle in 2 Timothy 4:8, for after affirming, 'I have kept the faith', he added, 'Henceforth there is laid up for me the crown of righteousness, which the Lord, the righteous judge will award to me on that Day, and not only to me but also to all who have loved his appearing.'

Such a confidence may be enjoyed by Christians without office in the church, as is plainly taught in Hebrews 6:10: 'God is not so unjust as to overlook your work and the love that you showed for his sake in serving the saints, as you still do.' The same epistle has a relevant message to believers who, though they lose earthly possessions, know they have a better and enduring possession in heaven: 'Therefore do not throw away your confidence, which has a great reward. For you have need of endurance' (*Heb*.10:35–36).

11

The Church of the Living God

I hope to come to you soon, but I am writing these things to you so that, [15] if I delay, you may know how one ought to behave in the household of God, which is the church of the living God, a pillar and buttress of truth. [16] Great indeed, we confess, is the mystery of godliness: He was manifested in the flesh, vindicated by the Spirit, seen by angels, proclaimed among the nations, believed on in the world, taken up in glory (1 Tim. 3:14–16).

This brief section is largely concerned with the nature of the church and the glory of the truth entrusted to her. It serves to emphasize the importance of the preceding chapters concerning her worship and her ministry. There is what may appear a studied casualness in the manner in which the apostle introduces this important theme, in that he mentions his hope to visit Timothy soon, at which time he would be able to direct the life of the church in Ephesus himself. The fact of writing, however, does enforce the need and urgency of putting the apostle's directions into operation, and in God's wise providence this passage has preserved for all the Christian churches through the centuries the Lord's own authoritative rules in this important realm.

Paul did not know when the unfolding of the will of God would take him to Ephesus. It might have been earlier than expected. But he did know that God was commanding him to pass on to Timothy the charge that he was writing. God's purpose would then be fulfilled, even if Paul were delayed by some unforeseen circumstances. In 1 Corinthians 4:19 he had shown his submission to God's will: 'I will come to you soon, if the Lord wills.' This exemplifies the direction of James 4:15, that we should not presume on the future but say, 'If the Lord wills we will live and do this or that.'

Though Timothy had the awesome responsibility of supervising the implementation of God's charge to him, we cannot regard this charge as restricted to his own conduct, for the clause has a wider remit concerning 'how [any] one should behave himself in the household of God' (verse 15). The translation *household* may be preferable to *house* since it denotes the people of God rather than a building where they assemble for worship. In the Old Testament the term 'house of God' very often refers to the temple as the place where God meets with his worshipping people (*2 Chron.* 5:14), but when God speaks of 'my house' it can also denote the covenant people of God (*Num.* 12:7). This aspect is apparent in Hebrews 3:5–6 where we read that just as Moses was faithful to God in his house as a servant, so Christ is faithful as a Son over God's house, which we believers are. Believers are members of God's household (*Eph.* 2:19) and when they assemble in their congregations for worship they constitute God's sanctuary, in which the Spirit of God dwells (*1 Cor.* 3:16).

The 'house of God' is further defined in terms of its spiritual glory as *the church of the living God*, that is, a living community in union with God, for Christians, as living stones, are being built up as a spiritual house (*1 Pet.* 2:5). The description *living* serves to distinguish the true God from all the false and unreal deities of the many other existing religions. The phrase recalls 1 Thessalonians 1:9 where conversion is described as turning 'to God from idols to serve the living and true God'. As the living God, he is the source of spiritual eternal life in believers, granting them real present fellowship with himself and sustaining that life until its consummation in heaven.

The term 'church' may denote a particular local congregation, as in Romans 16:1, 5, 'the church at Cenchreae' and 'the church in their [Prisca and Aquila's] house', but it can also refer to all the Christians in a city that may have included more than one congregation, 'the church of God that is in Corinth' (*1 Cor.* 1:2), or in a larger geographical area as in Acts 9:31, 'the church throughout all Judea and Galilee and Samaria'. (Some Greek texts, however, have the plural here, 'churches', as in 'the churches of Galatia', *Gal.* 1:2). This usage reflects the larger concept of the universal church as the body of Christ, of which he is the Head (*Eph.* 1:22,

Col. 1:18), for this is the church he loved and for which he gave himself as a sacrifice (*Eph.* 5:23, 25). The Lord Jesus Christ, as he promised, continues to build her (*Matt.* 16:18), by adding those who are being saved (*Acts* 2:47).

The great privileges and solemn responsibilities of all members of Christ's church are depicted in this description of her as *a pillar and buttress of truth*, for it means that the Christian church as a whole, and each local church, is responsible for upholding and defending the truth.

A *pillar* or column holds up the roof of a building and just as the columns lifted up the shining marble roof of the temple of Artemis at Ephesus so the church must hold aloft Christian doctrine to draw the attention of outsiders to the true and living God.

The Greek word *hedraioma* is only found here in the New Testament and, since Paul elsewhere uses a different noun for foundation, it is probably correct here to recognize its distinct meaning of *buttress* or bulwark, that which gives stability and firmness to a building. John Calvin commented on this: 'The office of administering doctrine, which God has placed in her [the church's] hands, is the only instrument of preserving the truth, that it may not perish from the remembrance of men.'

As the church functions aright in these capacities, according to the commands already given, she will prevent her life being ruined under the pressure of false teaching and her unity being broken by schismatic tendencies. This lofty conception of the church explains and emphasizes the need to implement fully and correctly the solemn charge previously recorded, so that she will highly commend the Lord Jesus Christ himself as her Head. Each church should aim to be stronger in the faith and purer in life in order to reveal to the on-looking world the glory and infinite value of the Saviour. The sad conclusion that must be drawn when a company of professing Christians does not uphold the fundamental doctrines of the faith is that it thereby relinquishes the claim to belong to the church of the living God.

In verse 16 we find the basic elements of revealed truth about the Lord Jesus Christ that are to be proclaimed and defended by the church and therefore require our own careful study. They are introduced in a striking manner: 'Great indeed, we confess, is the

[63]

mystery of godliness.' This emphasizes that this is the truth confessed by believers on the basis of scriptural revelation, and it is
beyond any doubt and without controversy among true Christians.
Paul had written earlier that his responsibility to make the Word of
God fully known included the teaching of this mystery, for 'God
chose to make known how great . . . are the riches of the glory of
this mystery, which is Christ in you, the hope of glory' (*Col.* 1:27).
In that letter (Colossians) he sets forth the sovereign lordship of
Christ and his all-sufficiency as Saviour, and the verse before us
similarly focuses on those fundamental truths. The genuine intellectual grasp of this mystery will always be accompanied by and
expressed in conscientious devotion to the Lord Jesus Christ.

Though it is widely taught that the apostle proceeds to quote
from a Christian hymn that was already circulating among the
churches, this is not indicated in the context. There seems to be
no reason why the verse should not be attributed to Paul. It would
be no surprise that a skilled communicator of the truth, under the
tuition of the Holy Spirit, should wisely use this form and style
to make these truths more readily remembered. Be that as it may,
now that it has been written down in this epistle it clearly has apostolic and therefore divine authority. This makes it necessary as well
as profitable to consider each element of it most carefully.

The AV and NKJV have preserved the word 'God' as the subject of
the verb, in accord with many Greek manuscripts that underlie the
so-called Textus Receptus, or 'Majority text', but textual critics
for more than a century have generally preferred the reading 'who'
or 'he'. It is not possible to pursue the textual arguments here, but
if we adopt the pronouns 'who' or 'he', an antecedent noun is obviously implied, and the sense required is, 'God was manifested in
the flesh.' There is no doubt that this verse refers to the Son of
God of whom Paul has previously written, 'Christ Jesus came into
the world to save sinners' (1:15; see comments on that verse).

The verb here translated *manifested* in the passive voice means
'made visible' and teaches that this person who is invisible in
his divine nature (1:17) has revealed himself in the flesh. This is
referred to in 1 John 1:2: 'The eternal life, which was with the
Father, was made manifest.' The term *the flesh* here means more
than a body. It denotes all that constitutes a human being, as we

read in John 1:14, 'The Word [which 'was with God' and 'was God'] became flesh and dwelt among us, and we beheld his glory, the glory as of the only begotten of the Father' (AV). The biblical teaching on the Person of Christ was clarified and well stated at the Council of Chalcedon, AD 451, where false ideas were also refuted: 'We all with one consent teach men to confess one and the same Son, our Lord Jesus Christ, the same perfect in Godhead and also perfect in manhood; truly God and truly man . . . We confess that one and the same Christ, Lord, and only-begotten Son, is to be acknowledged in two natures without confusion, change, division, or separation.' This was maintained through the centuries by the Christian church and was received by the Reformers as warranted by the testimony of Scripture. In these days, when this truth is under attack, Christians need to be convinced of its great value. Jesus Christ is true God and true man, in two distinct natures, yet one Person.

Jesus Christ, God *manifested in the flesh*, was *vindicated* in the sense that his claims to be the Son of God and the promised Saviour were proven true by his ministry, and particularly in his resurrection. Our translation, like the AV, assumes that 'spirit' here means the Holy Spirit, and this would be very relevant since the public ministry of the Lord Jesus was subsequent to his anointing by the Spirit (*Acts* 10:38), and it was by the Spirit of God that he cast out demons (*Matt.* 12:28). In his commentary, Hendriksen maintains, 'But it was specially by means of *his resurrection from the dead* that the Spirit *fully* vindicated the claim of Jesus that he was the Son of God (*Rom.* 1:4)' (*New Testament Commentary: 1 & 2 Timothy and Titus*, Banner of Truth, 1960, p. 140). Certainly it is by the Holy Spirit that God reveals who Jesus truly is (*1 Cor.* 2:10, 12:3), and thus certifies the testimony borne to him.

John Calvin explained, 'Under the word *spirit* he includes everything in Christ that was divine and superior to man, because his glory was almost wholly spiritual.' This view can be supported by an apparent contrast between *flesh* and *spirit*.

The next clause, *seen by angels*, or, more precisely, he *appeared* or *showed himself* to angels, probably refers specifically to his incarnate life. The Scriptures record some occasions. When the Lord Jesus was born, first one angel announced the fact to the shepherds, and then a multitude joined in the praise of God: 'Glory to God in the highest, and on earth peace, good will toward men' (*Luke* 2:14, AV). However the gospels also record the presence of angels after Jesus' temptations in the wilderness (*Matt.* 4:11), and Luke 22:43 records that an angel appeared to Jesus in the Garden of Gethsemane strengthening him. The testimony of angels to the fact of his resurrection is found in all four Gospels. Almost certainly we can also identify as angels the men in white robes who explained to the eleven at Jesus' ascension that he had been received up into heaven and would come again (*Acts* 1:10–11).

Jesus Christ was *proclaimed among the nations*, as he had commanded (*Mark* 16:15), for it was necessary that 'repentance and forgiveness of sins should be proclaimed in his name to all nations' (*Luke* 24:47). Paul had been commissioned by God to preach to the Gentiles the unsearchable riches of Christ (*Eph.* 3:8), since this had always been his purpose, as intimated in many Old Testament prophecies, like Joel 2:32, cited by Peter in Acts 2:21, and by Paul in Romans 10:13. More fully, in Romans 16:25–26, Paul speaks of his gospel and the preaching of Jesus Christ as being 'according to the revelation of the mystery that was kept secret for long ages but has now been disclosed and through the prophetic writings has been made known to all nations, according to the command of the eternal God'.

He was *believed on*, or trusted, *in the world*, and by this means the purpose of his coming into the world, to save sinners (1:15), was realized. The world here is a general term for mankind rather than explicitly the world in its hostility to God, and so conforms to its use in John 3:17: 'God did not send his Son into the world to condemn the world, but in order that the world might be saved through him.' 2 Thessalonians 1:10 records an instance of this: Paul's testimony to the Lord Jesus Christ was believed in Thessalonica, where the gospel had come in power and in the Holy Spirit (*1 Thess.* 1:5). Since faith comes from hearing and hearing through the word of Christ (*Rom.* 10:17), the proclamation of these truths concerning Christ is the outworking of God's design, for how shall the world hear and believe in him without a preacher (*Rom.* 10:14)?

The last clause, *taken up in glory*, refers to the historical event of Jesus' ascension, spoken of in John 20:17 and recorded in Mark

16:19, Luke 24:51, and Acts 1:2,11. Now he has gone into heaven and is at the right hand of God (*1 Pet.* 3:22, *Acts* 2:33), rightfully returning to the glory that was eternally his.

The movement from the opening reference to his incarnation to the closing reference to his exaltation is reflected on in Philippians 2:6–11. The One who is essentially God and came in the likeness of men humbled himself, becoming obedient to the point of death on a cross. Therefore God has highly exalted him and bestowed on him the name that is above every name. God the Father, who raised him from the dead, has given him glory (*1 Pet.* 1:21), and he will come again with his Father's glory (*Matt.* 16:27, 24:30).

The passage enlarges and enriches our understanding of the Person and ministry of the Lord Jesus and so prompts our adoration of him as our Saviour. But it should also stimulate our concern that he be honoured in his church, and by our testimony to him.

12

A Warning of Imminent
Departure from the Faith

*Now the Spirit expressly says that in later times some will depart
from the faith by devoting themselves to deceitful spirits and teachings of demons, ² through the insincerity of liars whose consciences are
seared, ³ who forbid marriage and require abstinence from foods that
God created to be received with thanksgiving by those who believe
and know the truth. ⁴ For everything created by God is good and
nothing is to be rejected if it is received with thanksgiving, ⁵ for it is
made holy by the word of God and prayer* (1 Tim. 4:1–5).

In his commentary, John Calvin has given incisive expression to
the over-riding purpose of this section:

> Paul forewarns not only the Ephesians, but all the churches
> throughout the world about hypocritical teachers, who by set-
> ting up false worship and by ensnaring consciences with new
> laws adulterate the true worship of God and corrupt the pure
> doctrine of faith.

There is a link, indicated by *Now*—perhaps better translated
'But'—with the preceding verse, 3:16, where Paul has set out vital
truths concerning the person and mission of the Lord Jesus Christ.
Though the church is the pillar and buttress of truth, serious error
will be taught within her congregations, and all Christians need to
be aware of this sad fact. It is introduced in the most forceful terms
as a specific message given by the Holy Spirit, probably to Paul
himself, that this will occur in the near future, that is, *in later times*,
rather than 'in the last days'.

The Lord Jesus himself had warned that false prophets would
arise and lead many astray (*Matt.* 24:11), and Paul had previously

told the Ephesian elders of this real danger (*Acts* 20:29–30), but what is now presented appears to be a recent and precise revelation of the Holy Spirit. Seven times in Revelation, chapters 2 and 3, the Lord insists, 'He who has an ear, let him hear what the Spirit says to the churches', and this remains as a Christian responsibility today.

The verb *depart* is the root of our word 'apostasy', a term now employed to denote the most serious departure from the faith, that is, from the revealed truths of Christian doctrine. This unbelieving abandonment of scriptural truth is traced to the influence of evil spirits who deceive men by means of human agents, as they spread teachings that have a demonic origin. It is important to recognize that the devil has from the beginning questioned the truth and the authority of God's words (*Gen.* 3:1–5). In Revelation 12:9, he is given the title, 'the deceiver of the whole world'. In 1 John 4:1, Christians are lovingly commanded to test the spirits, because many false prophets have gone out into the world. They are not naively to believe anything that human teachers say but to test it by the apostolic teaching.

Though these damnable, destructive heresies have a devilish origin, they are normally taught, not directly by demons but by the devil's human agents, who are described as liars speaking insincerely. There is an illustration of this in 1 Kings 22:22, where the faithful prophet Micaiah warned that a lying spirit had moved the false prophets to deceive Ahab, King of Israel, in contrast with the true message the Lord had given to Micaiah himself. Paul had written in 2 Corinthians 11:13–15 of false apostles and called them deceitful workmen and the servants of Satan, and in Ephesians 6:11 he taught the necessity of opposing them: 'Put on the whole armour of God, that you may be able to stand against the schemes of the devil.'

These teachers of unscriptural errors, spawned by the devil, are described as having their own consciences either *cauterized*, that is, made insensitive, or *branded*. If the latter sense of the verb is retained, such men are considered as aware of Satan's branding while they pretend a concern for holiness. The first meaning we have noted in our consideration of 1 Timothy 1:5. It denotes the result of stifling the warnings of conscience and resisting the voice of God in

Scripture. There is an implicit warning here against any attempt to exclude from our minds the teaching of God's Word that requires the response of faith and obedience. Rather we must heed the command of Hebrews 3:7, 'As the Holy Spirit says, "Today if you hear his voice, do not harden your hearts."' This quotation from Psalm 95:7 reminds us of the necessity of faith in God's promises, and the context in Hebrews cautions us against the hardening of the heart and disobedience. To maintain a clear and sensitive conscience, we should be quick and diligent to respond to all that God says to us, whenever we read his Word or hear it preached, 'Today . . . while it is called "today"' (*Heb*. 3:7,13)! God often reveals his concern at the consequences of failure to pay attention to his teaching. This is directly mentioned in Psalm 81:13, 'Oh, that my people would listen to me!'

Both the errors being taught by these apostates lie in the realm of ascetic practices, but they reflect serious doctrinal error about the goodness of God and the nature of true holiness. In *forbidding marriage* (verse 3) they directly opposed God's institution of the marriage bond, as seen in Genesis 2:22–24, when he brought Eve to Adam that they might be joined together as one flesh. This is confirmed by the Lord Jesus in Matthew 19:4–6. The sanctity of marriage is implied in the commandment, 'You shall not commit adultery.' It is also directly taught in Hebrews 13:4, 'Marriage is honourable in all and the bed undefiled.' I prefer this AV translation because it regards the sentence as a statement and not an exhortation.

It is a great mistake to exalt celibacy as if it were a superior moral and spiritual condition to that of marriage, for that is an implied criticism of God's command to be fruitful and multiply (*Gen*. 1:28). John Murray has expressed this well: 'Procreation is the divine institution and the procreative impulse is native to man' (*Principles of Conduct*, Eerdmans, 1991, p. 47). Of course the interests of godliness must be paramount in the marriage relationship; the husband must love his wife, and she must respect her husband (*Eph*. 5:33). Whenever marriage is forbidden and celibacy enforced, as it is on Roman Catholic clergy, there is a repudiation of the sole authority of the Lord Jesus over his church, and it is therefore not surprising that it often has sad consequences. However Jesus taught clearly that some may not be able to enter into marriage and some may voluntarily remain unmarried for the kingdom of heaven's sake (*Matt.* 19:12). Also, in 1 Corinthians 7:7,9 Paul teaches that the ability to be celibate is a divine gift, and adds that it is better for those without it to marry.

The prohibition of certain foods or the commanding of times of fasting (verse 3) has no divine sanction in the New Testament, for Christians are taught to recognize that God himself is the Provider of all food suitable for human consumption and for man's physical health. It is important to recall that it is expressly written in Genesis 1:12 that the various kinds of vegetation that the earth brought forth at the command of God are good in his esteem.

In Psalm 104:14 it is directly affirmed of the Lord God, 'You cause the grass to grow for the livestock and plants for man to cultivate, that he may bring forth food from the earth, and wine to gladden the heart of man, oil to make his face shine, and bread to strengthen man's heart.' It is the Lord who established seed-time and harvest (*Gen.* 8:22) and who gives men food in due season (*Psa.* 145:15). Also in Genesis 9:3 God sanctioned the eating of animal flesh, and this was clearly done in biblical times. Arbitrary restrictions on Christians' God-given liberty both deprive them of the nourishment he provides for their bodies and deny him their return of the thanks that he deserves. E. K. Simpson commented, 'God's gifts are suited to man's appetites and should be received with gratitude, not thrust aside in disdain. Believers are especially entitled to them because of their filial relationship to the Giver.'

Voluntary fasting for specific purposes is not however wrong in itself, for it was practised in the church at Antioch when the leaders sought God's direction regarding the missionary expedition of Barnabas and Saul (*Acts* 13:2). Jesus fasted before being tempted by the devil (*Matt.* 4:2), and he taught that secret fasting could have spiritual benefit, for, 'Your Father who sees in secret will reward you' (*Matt.* 6:18).

There are times when fasting may assist a person's concentration in prayer and so have great benefit, but normally as God gives us food we must be concerned in eating and drinking to glorify him (*1 Cor.* 10:31). Just as the Lord Jesus Christ has taught his disciples to pray to their Father in heaven, 'Give us this day our daily bread' (*Matt.* 6:11, *Luke* 11:3), so here in verse 3 they are encouraged to follow his practice of giving thanks for food (*Matt.* 15:36). This verse makes it clear that it is part of Christian duty to give sincere thanks to God at mealtimes in a way that accords with scriptural practice and so to acknowledge his great and undeserved goodness. The apostle Paul did this on the fourteenth day of a severe storm on the Mediterranean Sea as a testimony to his faith in God, when he urged his fearful fellow passengers to take nourishment:

> He took bread, and giving thanks to God in the presence of all he broke it and began to eat. Then they all were encouraged and ate some food themselves (*Acts* 27:35–36).

When Christians eat their food with grateful thanks to God they consecrate it for a holy purpose, for their bodies are holy in the sense that they belong to God by creation and redemption.

John Calvin comments perceptively and critically, 'It is a beastly thing when we sit down at table without any prayer, and when we have eaten to the full depart in utter forgetfulness of God.'

13

The Importance of True Godliness

If you put these things before the brothers, you will be a good servant of Christ Jesus, being trained in the words of the faith and of the good doctrine that you have followed. ⁷ Have nothing to do with irreverent silly myths. Rather train yourself for godliness; ⁸ for while bodily training is of some value, godliness is of value in every way, as it holds promise for the present life and also for the life to come. ⁹ The saying is trustworthy and deserving of full acceptance. ¹⁰ For to this end we toil and strive, because we have our hope set on the living God, who is the Saviour of all people, especially of those who believe (1 Tim. 4:6–10).

This section is another apostolic direction to Timothy for the fulfilment of his task at Ephesus and provides a pattern of Christian ministry that is relevant for all times. He is to instruct other Christians, who are called his brothers in Christ as a reminder that this must be done in true brotherly love. We presume that by *these things* Paul refers at least to the first five verses of this chapter, but probably they include all the relevant previous teaching in this epistle. They are to be *put before* his fellow-believers for their profit. It is possible, keeping the basic meaning of this verb, to suggest that these truths are to be laid down as a foundation for their faith and conduct. However more is required from a good servant of Christ Jesus than teaching others, and Timothy is required to train or nourish himself continually by means of the words of the Christian faith and sound, excellent doctrine that he has carefully followed.

This good teaching Timothy had heard from the apostle, as mentioned in 2 Timothy 3:10, and he was commanded in 2 Timothy 2:2 to commit those things to faithful men. The verb translated *follow* is used in Luke 1:3 where it implies thorough investigation of facts. This reminds all ministers that, like Timothy, they need to be very diligent in the reading and study of Scripture to gain the clearest and fullest understanding of its truths. The warning of William Hendriksen based on this text is quite challenging: 'A minister who neglects to study his Bible and the doctrine based upon it *atrophies* his powers by disuse' (*New Testament Commentary: 1 & 2 Timothy and Titus*, Banner of Truth, 1960, p. 150).

Besides the prayerful study of God's Word there must be the *training of oneself for godliness* (verse 7). This is contrasted with the false hopes of progress in godliness by means of the asceticism criticized in verse 3. The restrictive regulations, 'Do not handle, Do not taste, Do not touch', which may have an appearance of wisdom, are completely without value—indeed useless—in the realm of a man's sanctification (*Col.* 2:21–23).

It is necessary also in the exercise of a Christ-honouring ministry to avoid *irreverent, silly myths*, 'old wives' fables', that may fascinate and delude the uninstructed Christian. Timothy must totally reject them for what they are, mere fables of human speculation, and repudiate their claim to a hearing within the congregation. In our day, for example, adult Christians need to be warned against encouraging children to heed the popular myths about Santa Claus, since they will thereby be deluded and their attention diverted from the glorious truth of the love of God the Father in sending his Son to become the Saviour they need!

Positively Paul teaches the pressing need to exercise oneself in the realm of *godliness*. This requires self-control, like the rigorous discipline of mind and body of the athlete who wants to succeed in his contest. The language that Paul employs belongs to gymnastics. Among the Greeks young men would exercise themselves to achieve greater physical vigour and beauty of form to gain human approval. Christians should devote their time and energy to improving their spiritual lives by growth in grace and progress in true godliness to please God. In 1 Corinthians 9:24–27, Paul likened this endeavour to competing in athletic games, where every competitor exercised self-discipline in all things in order to win. Believers should do so in order to gain an incorruptible crown. He commends this by his own practice: 'I discipline my body and keep it under control.' Thereby he enforces the need to make our bodies serve our spiritual welfare.

The theme of *godliness* is found thirteen times in the Pastoral Epistles. The word denotes reverential awe of God, and in Christians this filial fear will always be accompanied by genuine love for God as Father. We have further guidance in Titus 2:11–12, where Paul teaches that the grace of God that brings salvation trains us 'to renounce ungodliness and worldly passions, and to live self-controlled, upright and godly lives in the present age'.

There is here (verse 8) a deliberate contrast with bodily exercise that has little profit because it is restricted to the physical realm, and makes no direct contribution to Christian development. This was included because of the problems that had arisen due to the commendation of ascetic conduct as conducing to spiritual maturity. It is still relevant, for such wrong ideas still find expression. Since our bodies belong to the Lord, however, we should try to preserve health and strength so that he is glorified in our use of them.

Just as diet plays a part in physical health so the Christian must nourish his soul by meditation on the healthy doctrine found in God's Word, inwardly digesting its truths and then living in the light and power of them. 'Receive with meekness the implanted word, which is able to save your souls. But be doers of the word, and not hearers only' (*James* 1:21–22).

There are no limits to the value of godliness. It is profitable in every way at all times, both during this *present life* on earth and for that which is *to come*. This benefit lies in that it brings close intimacy of fellowship with God and fosters the assurance that he is always with us, enabling us to be content in all circumstances (*Heb.* 13:5). This is the believer's testimony, found in Psalm 73:23–24. When he was experiencing physical distress and mental bewilderment the Psalmist affirmed, 'Nevertheless, I am continually with you; you hold my right hand. You guide me with your counsel, and afterwards you will receive me to glory.'

As an encouragement to Timothy to exercise himself to godliness the apostle adds (verse 9) that this is a *trustworthy saying* that deserves wholehearted *acceptance* by all. It implies that those who obediently comply will prove the blessing of godliness. This confirmation of the counsel given is most appropriate, since unbelievers repudiate it and believers are tempted to doubt it because progress in godliness may be accompanied by extra difficulties: 'All who desire to live a godly life in Christ Jesus will be persecuted' (*2 Tim.* 3:12).

Paul next (verse 10) includes Timothy with himself and probably other mature Christians in the *we* who already *toil and strive* at making progress in godliness because they have their *hope set on the living God*. The verb *toil* means to work with the kind of effort that brings fatigue. It is used of agricultural labour in 2 Timothy 2:6, but also by Paul of his labours as an apostle (*1 Cor.* 15:10), and of some who laboured in the church at Thessalonica (*1 Thess.* 5:12).

Instead of the verb translated here *strive*, there is an alternative in the Majority text which gives rise to the AV rendering, 'suffer reproach', a sense that would not be unsuitable here, for those who strive after holiness are often mocked by the world. However, the word translated *strive*, the root of the English word 'agonize', is used by Paul and joined to *toil* in Colossians 1:29: 'I toil, struggling with all his [Christ's] energy that he powerfully works within me'; and his testimony in 2 Timothy 4:7 uses the verb and its cognate noun: 'I have fought the good fight.'

This teaching takes up the theme of conflict introduced in 1:18. It is costly and difficult, but as believers engage in it they are granted wisdom and strength from the living God in whom they have set their hope firmly and consistently. Like Paul they too look forward to receiving the crown of righteousness from the Lord (*2 Tim.* 4:8), because their Lord Jesus Christ and God their Father has given them 'eternal comfort [encouragement] and good hope through grace' (*2 Thess.* 2:16).

The two-fold description of God in verse 10 serves to emphasize the wisdom and security of this hope. He is *the living God*, who spoke to his chosen people at Sinai (*Deut.* 5:26), and gives and sustains the life of his children, being steadfast forever as the sovereign ruler over all (*Dan.* 6:26). God is also *the Saviour of all people* and, as previously explained (see comments on 1 Timothy 1:1; 2:3), we recognize that this term was commonly used of a benefactor, so that even the emperor Nero could be called, 'Saviour of the inhabited world'.

We regard what is said here as emphasizing that God is good and does good to all kinds of men (*Psa.* 119:68), and that the earth is full of the goodness of the LORD (*Psa.* 33:5). The Lord is called the Saviour of Israel in the context of his providential activity on their behalf – not only in redemption from Egypt but also in supply of their physical needs in the wilderness (*Exod.* 14:30, *Psa.* 106:21; *Psa.* 107:13).

The additional phrase, *especially of those who believe*, focuses on the special relationship God has established by his grace with all who believe on the Lord Jesus Christ, for it is by grace we are saved, through faith (*Eph.* 2:8). We know that all things work together for good for those whom God has called, and he will certainly glorify them (*Rom.* 8:28–30), for the good work he has begun he will bring to completion (*Phil.* 1:6). The testimony of David in Psalm 138:8 can be shared by all believers, 'The LORD will fulfil his purpose for me; your steadfast love, O LORD, endures for ever.'

14

Guidance for the Christian Ministry

Command and teach these things. ¹² Let no one despise you for your youth, but set the believers an example in speech, in conduct, in love, in faith, in purity. ¹³ Until I come, devote yourself to the public reading of Scripture, to exhortation, to teaching. ¹⁴ Do not neglect the gift you have, which was given you by prophecy when the council of elders laid their hands on you. ¹⁵ Practise these things, devote yourself to them, so that all may see your progress. ¹⁶ Keep a close watch on yourself and on the teaching. Persist in this, for by so doing you will save both yourself and your hearers (1 Tim. 4:11–16).

It is difficult to determine the extent of *these things* (verse 11). Since the phrase is found in verse 6, it could be restricted to the intervening section, but the previous occurrence of the phrase in 3:14 probably warrants the inclusion of all the instruction given after that. Timothy is required to continue his responsibility to command (see 1:3) and to teach the truths entrusted to him as the servant of God with authority, for God purposed by this means to bring the hearers into submission to himself. It is pertinent to realize that the minister should not be offering his opinions for discussion, nor making suggestions for men's approbation, but declaring God's truth, which all should receive with meekness and benefit from (*James* 1:21, *Heb.* 4:2). Proficiency in teaching necessitates both painstaking effort to understand the Scripture and wisdom in expounding and applying its truth to its hearers, and Paul supplements this aspect in the following verses.

There was a danger that because of his *youth*—the term probably indicates that Timothy was between thirty-five and forty years old by this time—some would *despise* his ministry (verse 12), even push him aside, for the verb often implies action and not merely mental attitude. Timothy was not to respond by asserting his authority but by being a good role model for all Christians. His character and *conduct* should commend his teaching. He had already been a good example when with Paul at Thessalonica, for they had given the believers there 'an example to imitate' (*2 Thess.* 3:9), and he must continue to be an exemplary pattern of Christian living.

Speech here almost certainly extends beyond his teaching to all that he says and this accords with the counsel given to all Christians in Colossians 4:6, 'Let your speech always be gracious, seasoned with salt.' Nothing should be said that conflicts with his Christian profession or brings disrepute on his office. Neither foolish talking nor coarse jesting ought to have any place in his conversation (*Eph.* 5:4). Beside speech, the whole of Timothy's *conduct* should be above reproach, for as it is said, 'Actions speak louder than words', and unless his observable behaviour conforms to what he says men will consider him a hypocrite.

Paul then turns from what can be heard or seen by others to inward dispositions and not surprisingly he first mentions *love*, for this is not a quiescent but a dynamic virtue, and its exercise is the basic evidence that anyone is a disciple of Christ (*John* 13:35). The love of the Lord Jesus is both the pattern and the motivation of believers' love—'We love because he first loved us' (*1 John* 4:19)—and when this love is genuine it will be active: 'Let us not love in word or talk but in deed and in truth' (*1 John* 3:18).

Faith here could have the active meaning of believing, for every Christian needs continually to exercise faith or trust in God. This was a characteristic of Stephen, who was 'full of faith' (*Acts* 6:5). Hebrews 11 has a number of examples of such faith, described in verse 1 as 'the assurance of things hoped for, the conviction of things not seen'.

Just as the Greek noun for faith is occasionally used of God (see *Rom.* 3:3), and translated 'faithfulness', so here the meaning may be that Timothy should be trustworthy or reliable, for faithfulness is joined to love as the fruit of the Spirit (*Gal.* 5:22).We should perhaps recognize the latitude of meaning here, for genuine faith in God will always tend to produce faithfulness: 'They who are trustful are trusty also' (J. B. Lightfoot, *St Paul's Epistle to the Galatians*, 2nd ed., 1866, p. 153).

The last mentioned quality is that of *purity*. This must begin within the heart and then find expression in word and conduct, and Timothy is further exhorted in 5:22, 'Keep yourself pure.' This requires inner discipline to remove and overcome impurity of thought and motive, for he who has his hope fixed on the Lord Jesus Christ 'purifies himself as he is pure' (*1 John* 3:3). When these characteristics are evident in his life, Timothy will be preserved from the disdain that others—older Christians especially—might feel towards him as a relatively young man.

At verse 13, Paul moves on from Christian character to ministerial responsibility. This order is significant. It is reflected in the qualifications for elders. There must be real holiness of life as the basis for the exercise of ministry that is acceptable to God.

In the interval before Paul arrives, Timothy must commit himself to certain tasks within the life of the church. Though he needed to read and ponder God's Word for himself, it is probable that the reference here is to *the public reading of Scripture* in the services of the church. This was a normal feature of synagogue worship, as we see from Luke 4:16–17, and Acts 13:15—'the reading from the Law and the Prophets'. The noun was often used in secular Greek of the public reading of documents. The reading of the Scriptures became a regular element in the worship services of the early church, according to Justin Martyr who wrote around AD 140 that 'the memoirs of the apostles [the Gospels] or the writings of the prophets [from the Old Testament] are read for as long as time permits'. The reading was followed by instruction and exhortation. This included both the Gospels and other parts of the New Testament as we now have it, but in Timothy's time it would have been largely the Old Testament. However we note in Colossians 4:16 the command, 'When this letter has been read among you, have it also read in the church of the Laodiceans', and Paul's letters are given the same authority as other Scriptures (*2 Pet.* 3:16). When there were few copies of the Scriptures it was obviously necessary that they should be read publicly, as indicated in Revelation 1:3, 'Blessed is the one who reads aloud . . . and blessed are those who hear.' From Revelation 2 and 3 it is plain that Christians from the seven churches were expected to hear what the Spirit was saying by reading or hearing the letters sent to them all.

As Timothy was to give attention to the public reading of Scripture, so it is necessary today that in congregational worship this is done with clarity and due reverence, acknowledging that it is the Word of God.

Exhortation carries the sense of appeal to the heart and conscience of the hearers, with the aim of stimulating a positive response to the truth. It includes relevant encouragement or comfort. Paul wrote in Romans 15:4 that Bible truths were written 'for our instruction, that . . . through the encouragement [exhortation] of the Scriptures we might have hope'.

The noun *teaching* probably here focuses on the activity rather than the content, but of course it would be the *sound doctrine* mentioned in 1:10 that Timothy was expected to teach. This is the proclamation of the profound and precious truths of Holy Scripture so that the hearers may understand and benefit. Both *teaching* and *exhortation* are mentioned in Romans 12:7–8 as the exercise of valuable gifts in the church of the Lord Jesus Christ, warranted by God's Word.

Timothy is counselled (verse 14) not to neglect the grace-gift (*charisma*) given him by God for his ministry. It must be diligently cultivated and employed, and in 2 Timothy 1:6 he is required to fan it into flame, so that its fire may burn higher and more brightly. The Spirit who conveys this gift is the Spirit of power, and Timothy must aim to be filled with the Spirit (*Eph.* 5:18), to discharge his divinely-appointed mission.

Paul here mentions the outward accompaniments of the divine bestowal of the gift. The *prophecy* revealed God's authoritative guidance in Timothy's ordination. It is also referred to in 1:18. There is a parallel in Acts 13:2 when the prophets and elders at Antioch received God's direction. The Holy Spirit said, 'Set apart for me Barnabas and Saul for the work to which I have called them.' 'Then after fasting and praying they laid their hands on them and sent them off' (*Acts* 13:3). The fact that the body or *council of elders* (Greek: *presbuterion*) *laid their hands on* Timothy recalls the reference in Deuteronomy 34:9, 'Joshua . . . was full of the spirit of wisdom, for Moses had laid his hands on him', as the LORD had commanded (*Num.* 27:18). The laying on of hands has been preserved in the Christian church as warranted by Scripture. Though it cannot in itself convey divine grace, it is a suitable and divinely-appointed sign of the church's recognition that the minister has been called of God and equipped by him for the work.

Timothy is responsible to stir up the divine gift by responding to the commands of verse 15, completely *devoting himself* to his task. The translation *Practise these things* can be justified from contemporary writings as almost equivalent to 'exercise yourself in them'; but the verb used can also refer to meditative study, and the other use in the New Testament (in Acts 4:25, quoting Psalm 2:1), could mean either 'meditate' or 'devise'. Timothy must *devote himself* to them, literally 'be in them', that is, be wholly engrossed in them, so that nothing and no one can distract him from fulfilling his ministry, as Paul later charged him (*2 Tim.* 4:5). The apostle's command to Archippus in Colossians 4:17 has the same concern: 'See that you fulfil the ministry that you have received in the Lord.' This is echoed in the exhortation traditionally made to men seeking ordination in Protestant churches, that they should 'apply themselves wholly to this one thing, and draw all their cares and studies this way' (*Book of Common Prayer*).

By obeying these directives the progress of Timothy in both personal godliness and ministerial fitness would become apparent to all and thus commend him and his message even more widely.

There is further direction and encouragement in verse 16, *Keep a close watch on* yourself *and on the teaching*, for these are vitally connected in the work of the ministry, as previously intimated in verses 12–13. This injunction is similar to that given by Paul to the elders from Ephesus in Acts 20:28, 'Pay careful attention to yourselves and to all the flock, of which the Holy Spirit has made you overseers.' Timothy, and every elder, must continue in the exercise of inner discipline and consistent living as well as in the faithful teaching and application of God's Word, for this will be blessed of God in his own progress in salvation and in the salvation of those who hear him.

Timothy had been saved several years earlier, so that the verb *save* must include such progress, in accord with Philippians 2:12–13, 'Work out your own salvation with fear and trembling, for it is God who works in you, both to will and to work for his good pleasure.' The language of the apostle emphasizes that God, according to his own purpose, really does use those who teach Scripture-truth in the work of salvation. Accordingly, Paul wrote in 2 Corinthians 3:6 that his sufficiency was of God, 'who has made us [himself and Timothy] competent to be ministers' of the New Covenant. John Calvin helps us to avoid drawing the wrong conclusions from verse 16:

> It is God alone who saves; and not even the smallest portion of his glory can lawfully be bestowed on man. But God parts with no portion of his glory when he employs the agency of men for bestowing salvation.

The preacher is the living agent and God's Word ministered by him is the tool God is pleased to employ in bringing sinners into the enjoyment of salvation.

As Paul wrote in 1 Corinthians 4:15, 'In Christ Jesus I have begotten you through the gospel' (AV/NKJV). The ESV translation, 'I became your father', may sound rather strange, but can be understood in the light of the comparison Paul makes in the context between himself, as the one under whose ministry they were saved, and their many subsequent teachers or 'child-trainers'. He also describes Timothy in the same context as 'my beloved and faithful child in the Lord'.

15

Dealing with Church Members

Do not rebuke an older man, but encourage him as you would a father. Treat younger men like brothers, [2] older women like mothers, younger women like sisters, in all purity. [3] Honour widows who are truly widows. [4] But if a widow has children or grandchildren, let them first learn to show godliness to their own household and to make some return to their parents, for this is pleasing in the sight of God. [5] She who is truly a widow, left all alone, has set her hope on God and continues in supplications and prayers night and day, [6] but she who is self-indulgent is dead even while she lives. [7] Command these things as well, so that they may be without reproach. [8] But if anyone does not provide for his relatives, and especially for members of his household, he has denied the faith and is worse than an unbeliever (1 Tim. 5:1–8).

Underlying these directions is an understanding and appreciation of the Christian church as the family of God. This must govern the way in which Timothy and ministers generally deal with members as they teach and, where necessary, discipline them, to promote their growth in grace. It is indeed important that all Christians should view their fellow-believers as equally sons and daughters of God the Father, redeemed by the precious blood of Christ, and born again of the Holy Spirit. We may note that in their writings the apostles often call Christians 'beloved', as in 1 John 3:2: 'Beloved, we are God's children now.' This recognition will encourage real fellowship, and the stirring up of one another to love and good works (*Heb.* 10:24).

Paul begins with a caution: *Do not rebuke an older man.* The verb is found nowhere else in the New Testament. It has overtones of severity and sharpness and it is this element that would be inappropriate, while the general principle of convicting and rebuking from

God's Word (*2 Tim.* 4:2), must be consistently and impartially applied. The positive action is well conveyed by the translation, *encourage.* However, it is plain from the use of the verb in the New Testament that this may include both giving comfort when someone is sad or troubled, and exhorting, that is, strongly urging someone to do something, when they need to be stimulated to make progress in their exercise of faith and love.

Though this encouragement is to be given to believers of all ages and both sexes, there is some distinction to be made. In speaking to *older men,* Timothy must treat them with the kind of respect owed to fathers, an attitude commended in Leviticus 19:32: 'You shall stand up before the grey head and honour the face of an old man, and you shall fear your God: I am the LORD.'

Younger men must be regarded as *brothers,* with affectionate concern for their spiritual welfare and the realization that their inexperience brings particular problems, as well as important opportunities to guide them in their development into maturity.

In his dealings with *older women* as *mothers,* the principle of Proverbs 23:22 should be applied: 'Do not despise your mother when she is old.' They should be encouraged particularly to continue in the distinct contributions they make in the life of the congregation and within the family. We note that Paul in Romans 16:13 sent his greetings to Rufus, and 'also his mother, who has been a mother to me as well', revealing his appreciation of this woman's help.

Younger women should also be encouraged in living the Christian life by dealing with them as *sisters* in the Lord, with understanding and relevant counsel. The additional phrase, *with all purity,* reminds Timothy that he should be an example in purity (4:12), and emphasizes his need to maintain the strictest purity of thought, word, and gesture in giving counsel to younger women. When a minister fails to heed this counsel the consequences are likely to be harmful to both, and so will bring shame on the church of Christ.

In verses 3–8 the apostle is concerned that Timothy himself should give *honour* to those who are *truly widows,* and commend this attitude within the church. It is important that a distinction is made among widows, for, though obviously all have been bereaved of their husbands, they are not in the same position regarding their need of provision.

Firstly, the apostle teaches that Christian children and grand-children of widows need to learn that they should show the genu-ineness of their *godliness*, or professed piety, in the context of their family relations. There is a real obligation to requite their mothers or grandmothers for all the kindness they have experienced from birth onwards, and to do so with genuine gratitude and apprecia-tion. It is often only when Christians have children themselves that they begin to recognize all that good parenting has cost their par-ents. This should prompt their devoted care, especially for wid-owed mothers. The discharge of this responsibility accords with the fifth commandment, 'Honour your father and your mother' (*Exod*. 20:12), referred to by Paul in Ephesians 6:1–2. It is therefore a duty in which they should seek to please God. We note that the Lord Jesus most strongly criticized the tradition promoted by the scribes and Pharisees that exempted children from honouring their fathers and mothers by declaring that the children's money was *Corban*, a gift to God (*Mark* 7:10–12). Clearly there the teaching of Jesus implies that giving honour to parents, especially widows, should include making practical contributions to their welfare.

However, it is not only family members but the congregation also that is to share in the honouring of widows who are destitute and desolate (*left all alone*, verse 5). We note that this was early prac-tised in Jerusalem (*Acts* 6:1) when a daily distribution was made to widows. Doubtless widows would have been included in the refer-ences in earlier chapters to those who had need (*Acts* 2:45; 4:34–35), for whose sake Christians sold their possessions and goods, with the result that there was no one among them that lacked. God's concern for widows is revealed in Psalm 68:5: 'Father of the father-less and protector of widows is God in his holy habitation'; and in Psalm 146:9: 'He upholds the widow and the fatherless.' God had commanded his chosen people to be his agents in giving relief by enabling the poor and widows to glean in their harvests of grain, olives and grapes (*Deut*. 24:19–21), and allowing them to eat and be satisfied from their produce (*Deut*. 14:29).

The church is commanded to provide for those widows who have been *left all alone*, that is, without any financial resources. They are characterized also by having set their hope in God, con-tinually relying on him, like David who affirmed, 'My expectation is from him' (*Psa.* 62:5). This trust in God is evidenced in the widow's perseverance in calling on him in *supplications*, expressing her needs, and in *prayers*, enjoying her fellowship with him.

It is significant that her confident *hope* did not rest on the church, and was not, it seems, expressed in begging from other Christians, but in making her needs known to God. Such behaviour recalls that of the elderly Anna who served God continually 'with fasting and prayer night and day'. She was privileged to enter the temple courts when the infant Jesus was there, and joined in giving thanks to God for him as the promised Redeemer (*Luke* 2:36–38).

There are others (verse 6) who are completely different and live in pleasure. The verb refers to a life of *self-indulgence*, marked by wasteful, if not immoral, conduct, like that of the prodigal son who squandered his wealth by pandering to his own desires (*Luke* 15:13,30). If they lacked the resources needed to sustain a reasonable lifestyle, many widows in the society of that time would have been tempted to resort to questionable, even immoral, means to provide for themselves. That kind of conduct does not deserve the name of living but is rather an evidence of spiritual death. This recalls the startling message given to the church in Sardis, 'You have the reputation of being alive, but you are dead' (*Rev.* 3:1). The proof of true life in Christ is activity in ongoing fellowship with him, whatever one's age or status, and in the exercise of Christian love. Paul's words are searching and can be applied as a warning against the danger that Christian men and women may regard retirement only as an opportunity to enjoy themselves, instead of a time in which they can serve the Lord and his church in different ways.

Timothy must *command these things* (verse 7), both for the sake of the church and for the widows themselves, so that in this matter of provision they may be *without reproach* from the world, and blameless before God.

This section is concluded in verse 8 by a solemn warning which, though linked directly to the support of widows, has a wider relevance in the realm of family relationships. Failure to make provision for needy relatives, especially close family, is a denial of the Christian faith professed, for true faith and love are inextricably joined together. Note 1 Timothy 1:5, and Galatians 5:6: 'faith working through love'. A man may say that he has faith, but if that faith is not expressed in deeds of love, it is dead. Then that profession is as lifeless as a body without breath or spirit (*James* 2:26).

The seriousness of wilful neglect of duties towards those joined to us by family ties is emphasized by the statement that the person guilty of it is *worse than an unbeliever*. Many without the light of scriptural revelation and the virtues implanted by the Holy Spirit do recognize what they regard as the bonds of nature and exercise those natural affections in providing for their older and needy family members. Indeed, in some heathen religions and in structures of society untouched by Christianity it is expected that the older generation will be honoured in this practical way. The language is so forceful that professing Christians should be greatly disturbed if they have failed to honour the Lord and commend the Christian faith in this matter, and ought to confess the fault before God and implore his grace and mercy.

16

Guidance for Enrolling Widows in the Church

Let a widow be enrolled if she is not less than sixty years old, having been the wife of one husband, ¹⁰ and having a reputation for good works: if she has brought up children, has shown hospitality, has washed the feet of the saints, has cared for the afflicted, and has devoted herself to every good work. ¹¹ But refuse to enrol younger widows; for when their passions draw them away from Christ, they desire to marry ¹² and so incur condemnation for having abandoned their former faith. ¹³ Besides that, they learn to be idlers, going about from house to house, and not only idlers, but also gossips and busybodies, saying what they should not. ¹⁴ So I would have younger widows marry, bear children, manage their households, and give the adversary no occasion for slander. ¹⁵ For some have already strayed after Satan. ¹⁶ If any believing woman has relatives who are widows, let her care for them. Let the church not be burdened, so that it may care for those who are really widows (1 Tim. 5:9–16).

The preceding paragraph has been concerned with making provision for widows, and now Paul moves on to give guidance about placing some widows on the church's list. The verb translated *enrolled* was used by secular writers of choosing and enrolling soldiers or workmen, and so here we may presume that it denotes enlisting for service connected with the church, and not only for benefit from her funds. The nature of that service is not explained, nor is there any specific title given to those enrolled, though in Acts 9:39, 41 mention is made of a group of widows who probably, like Dorcas, were occupied in charitable works including making tunics and garments. However, apart perhaps from the requirement about age, the qualifications set out for enrolment do provide important clues about the role they were to play in the life of the church.

The reason for the widow being *not less than sixty years of age* is partly linked with the experience she will have gained as a Christian and with the respect that her life will have earned, but it is also related to the exclusion of younger widows explained in verses 11–13.

To have been *the wife of one husband* could indicate that she had not sought remarriage after her first husband died, but this restriction does not seem to accord with the apostolic counsel in 1 Corinthians 7:39 that a widow is 'free to be married to whom she wishes, only in the Lord'. Probably, then, it emphasizes the fact that she had upheld the sanctity of Christian marriage, and was not guilty of adultery or otherwise breaking marriage vows.

This elderly widow should be recommended by other Christians for the consistently good quality of her conduct, particularly in the four aspects that are detailed next.

She must be experienced in the nurture of *children* presumably her own, and have *brought them up* in the discipline and instruction of the Lord (*Eph.* 6:4), as well as caring for their physical and social needs. This care includes 'nourishing' them, as another form of the verb is translated in Ephesians 5:29, an activity that would extend to their moral tuition and general education, since a compound form of the verb was used by Paul in Acts 22:3 of his education in Jerusalem.

This elderly widow will have been often engaged in giving *hospitality*, even when her husband was alive, and so will have been obedient to the command of Romans 12:13, 'Contribute to the needs of the saints and seek to show hospitality.'

The *washing of the feet* of visitors to the home was regarded as a normal part of considerate hospitality as noted in Luke 7:44, but it also betokened a willingness to humble oneself in the service of others. The Lord Jesus displayed this humility when he washed the feet of his disciples and then commended the practice to them: 'If I then, your Lord and Teacher, have washed your feet, you also ought to wash one another's feet. For I have given you an example, that you also should do just as I have done to you' (*John* 13:14–15). This, then, is an example of readiness to perform even the most menial of tasks for the members of God's family, and would often be connected with giving relief to those who are distressed.

Caring for the afflicted would include practical help at the material level, and ministering to physical, mental and social needs, including those accompanying old age. Such giving of comfort might involve entering into the grief of the afflicted: 'Weep with those who weep' (*Rom.* 12:15).

The list closes with a more comprehensive expression (*devoted herself to every good work*), denoting her thoroughgoing commitment to do what she could for the welfare of others.

There are no explicit details here about the purpose of this list, but the most natural conclusion is that these prayerful elderly widows were authorized to exercise their proven abilities to do good within the Christian community. The New Testament does not mention any official role for such widows, but the passage is an encouragement to them to engage in these activities that are so beneficial to the church. By the third century, there was in some churches a register of widows who gave themselves to prayer, nursed the sick, cared for orphans, evangelized women, and then taught them in the faith.

Though widows under sixty could not be enrolled, this surely did not mean that they should be excluded from the support of the church, since they could be the most needy, especially if they had young children. Since this is God's direction, we must own that it is wise and good, both for the congregation and for the widows concerned, and this is explained in the next verses. If a younger widow pledged herself to serve the Lord Jesus Christ in this way, she might well subsequently become restive under his yoke because of a strong desire to remarry, and remarriage, though not sinful in itself (*1 Cor.* 7:39–40), would mean renouncing her loyalty to Christ and bring her under judgment. *Condemnation* is probably too strong a word here. This kind of failure may be related to that warned against by the Lord Jesus in Luke 9:62, 'No one who puts his hand to the plough and looks back is fit for the kingdom of God.'

The second problem is that younger more lively widows might succumb to the temptation to become idle and spend their time *going about from house to house* as *gossips* and not as helpers in the spiritual or practical realm. Instead of being busy doing good, they might become *busybodies* who interfered improperly in others' affairs and were too talkative about private matters. The positive counsel given to younger widows is that if they desired they should marry, for this would provide them with the opportunity to have the joy of motherhood, under God's blessing, and to use their feminine skills in managing the life of the family. When they obeyed this apostolic counsel, both they and the church would avoid incurring the reproach of *the adversary*, probably not a reference to the devil, but to anyone who is opposed to the Christian faith.

Perhaps some at Ephesus might have felt that this age restriction and the comments about the potential failures of younger women were unfair, so Paul concludes (verse 15) with the statement that already some had turned away from Christ by succumbing to Satan's wiles. This teaching was given by God in order to avoid a real and present danger within the church, and it should be recognized as revealing his perfect love and wisdom, with implications for our days as well.

In the closing verse (verse 16) we have a restatement of the church's responsibility to support those who are *really widows*, who lack any other means or source of financial help. It is to facilitate this that all believers should provide all needed relief for widows who belong to their own families.

17

The Honour Due to Church Elders

Let the elders who rule well be considered worthy of double hon-
our, especially those who labour in preaching and teaching. [18] For
the Scripture says, 'You shall not muzzle an ox when it treads out
the grain', and, 'The labourer deserves his wages.' [19] Do not admit a
charge against an elder except on the evidence of two or three wit-
nesses. [20] As for those who persist in sin, rebuke them in the presence of
all, so that the rest may stand in fear. [21] In the presence of God and of
Christ Jesus Christ and of the elect angels I charge you to keep these
rules without prejudging, doing nothing from partiality. [22] Do not be
hasty in the laying on of hands nor take part in the sins of others; keep
yourself pure. [23] (No longer drink only water, but use a little wine
for the sake of your stomach and your frequent ailments.) [24] The sins
of some men are conspicuous going before them to judgement, but the
sins of others appear later. [25] So also good works are conspicuous, and
even those that are not cannot remain hidden (1 Tim. 5:17–25).

Here the reference is not to older men generally, as in 5:1, but
to church elders about whose qualifications for office Paul
has written in 3:1–7. Their general task is to *rule*, that is, to govern
or preside over the life of the church, and in 1 Thessalonians 5:12
Christians are told 'to respect those who labour among you and
are over you in the Lord'. Here it is taught that those who do so
properly are worthy of double honour, and though this may denote
both respect and support, the context seems to relate it directly
to the provision of material help, as with honouring true widows,
verse 3.

The adverb *well* is emphasized by its prominence and denotes
that the work is done with proficiency; and *labour* stresses the fact
that the work involves diligence that often leads to weariness of
body or mind.

This hard and tiring work lies both in the careful study of the Word of God and in the teaching of its truths, and Paul describes its nature in the command, 'Do your best [or, Be diligent] to present yourself to God as one approved, a worker who has no need to be ashamed, rightly handling the word of truth' (*2 Tim.* 2:15). This principle is stated in Romans 12:8: the one who has the grace-gift to lead or govern must exercise it with diligence. There seems to be an implied distinction between those who labour excellently in preaching the word and in teaching, and some who do not, though the implication may also be that some elders were not involved in this sphere of service. All elders must be 'able to teach' (3:2), but all are not fully committed to doing so regularly in the congregation. However, those who labour exclusively in this work must receive ample provision from those who benefit.

The church's duty to provide for hardworking elders is pressed home by Paul's quotation of authoritative scripture (*Deut.* 25:4). This verse refers directly to permitting an ox that is threshing to partake of the grain, but the principle applies with even more force to those who labour to provide spiritual nourishment for believers. This interpretation of the text is not at all fanciful but conveys the underlying concept that is here clarified under the inspiration of the Holy Spirit. Paul comments on this matter in greater detail in 1 Corinthians 9:9–14, where he adds that the spiritual benefit conveyed by biblical teaching is of much greater value than any return given in the material realm. He further teaches that, as God had appointed that those who served by his appointment in the temple should benefit materially from it, so should those who serve him in the Christian church: 'The Lord commanded that those who proclaim the gospel should get their living by the gospel.' This teaching accords with that given in Galatians 6:6, 'One who is taught the word must share all good things with the one who teaches.'

Paul adds another reason, 'The labourer deserves his wages.' These words are also found in Luke 10:7. They were spoken by the Lord Jesus to the seventy-two whom he sent out to preach the kingdom of God, as their warrant to receive food and drink from those who gave them hospitality. If, as seems probable, these words are also included in what 'the Scripture says' (verse 18), then we may conclude that the apostle acknowledges the Gospel according to Luke as part of God-breathed Scripture, on a par with the Old Testament. Not all commentators are willing to accept this conclusion. Some suggest that Paul's words are only a citation of a known principle, also referred to by Jesus; though, since it was not in fact a regular feature of the world's treatment of servants, this is doubtful. The placing of these words here, as in Luke's Gospel, sufficiently establishes and even emphasizes their divine authority.

The honour to be given to elders does not exempt them from criticism, and verses 19–20 deal with the sensitive subject of *a charge against an elder*, building on the principle taught in Deuteronomy 19:15, 'On the evidence of two witnesses or of three witnesses shall a charge be established.' It would be quite improper to receive an accusation made by one individual, and unnecessary to proceed to a judicial hearing, for elders who carefully apply divine standards in order to convict and correct their hearers are likely to stir up an adverse reaction. The Lord Jesus met with such a response to his teaching: 'You are a Samaritan and have a demon' (*John* 8:48), and he was accused falsely before Pilate in Luke 23:1.

Malicious rumours and unsubstantiated slander of God's chosen and faithful servants must be repudiated for the benefit, not only of the elders, but also of the church. John Calvin recognized in this the craftiness of Satan in trying to alienate Christians from their elders, thereby casting doubt on the authority of their biblical teaching. However, when any accusation is adequately supported, Timothy must investigate it thoroughly and, once the facts are discovered, make them known.

Though an elder, rightly accused, would be among their number, *those who persist in sin* (verse 20), literally 'the ones sinning', must include all who are found guilty. They must be *rebuked in the presence of all.* There is a positive and beneficial design in making the verdict public, for it should solemnly warn all church members to keep themselves from sin and walk in the fear of God. Obviously the sinful practices that are to be rebuked were not secret but in the open, and the discipline was also to be made public to honour God openly as one who is holy and righteous in all his ways.

When the offences are sufficiently serious, a more drastic judgment must be made for, according to the teaching of Titus 3:10–11, anyone who causes divisions within the church by false teaching

[95]

and by rejecting sound doctrine is to be rejected after two solemn warnings.

The apostle begins the next section (verses 21–25) with a most earnest and solemn charge, by which he emphasizes that Timothy must observe or guard these rules as conscious of the close scrutiny of God the Father and the Lord Jesus Christ. In 2 Timothy 4:1, a similar charge is given, but with a wider reference to his entire ministry, and it is supplemented by the reminder that the Lord will judge the living and the dead at his appearing. God the Father has given Jesus authority to execute judgment, because he is the Son of Man (*John* 5:27), and we must all appear before the judgment seat of Christ (*2 Cor.* 5:10).

Here mention is also made of *the elect angels*, distinguished by God's choice from those who sinned and did not keep their proper dwelling (*2 Pet.* 2:4, *Jude* 6). The holy angels will be associated with the Lord Jesus when he comes in glory (*Matt.* 25:31), and are all ministering spirits whom God has sent for the sake of those who are to inherit salvation (*Heb.* 1:14).

Timothy must respond to all the directions given to him *without prejudging,* but rather with a careful consideration of the facts, and avoiding any *partiality*, that is, leaning favourably to one side. This accords with the teaching of Proverbs 24:23, 'Partiality in judging is not good', and we note that even the enemies of the Lord Jesus Christ acknowledged that he spoke and taught rightly and showed no partiality (*Luke* 20:21).

The prohibition, *Do not be hasty in the laying on of hands* (verse 22), refers almost certainly to the ordination of elders, for this rite has recently been mentioned in 4:14, and it fits the present context admirably. Timothy, then, is counselled to take time assessing relevant information about a candidate for eldership, in the light of the guidance given in 3:1–7, before he proceeds to ordain him.

Paul adds another warning: that Timothy should be careful not to *take part in the sins of others.* Though this may include rashly ordaining an unsuitable man, it should not be restricted to that fault. Instead of any such rash actions, Timothy must continue to *keep himself pure* in heart, inwardly clean of any defilement, and also innocent of harming the church of the living God by failing to do his duty.

The counsel of verse 23 is not the imposition of a total ban on drinking water but is rather a warning against being a total abstainer from wine, for taking *a little wine* would preserve and enhance his bodily health for the exercise of his ministry. We note *a little wine*, in contrast with the 'much wine' of 3:8, for addiction to wine could result in the sin of drunkenness (3:3,8).

This counsel may be a deliberate denial of the asceticism practised among the Jewish sect called the Essenes and of the regulations criticized in Colossians 2:20–23, where the proscriptions, 'Do not handle, Do not taste, Do not touch', probably included total abstinence from alcoholic drink. Medical opinion in Paul's time and today concurs in the assessment that moderate wine drinking can be beneficial as a tonic or to help prevent or remedy some serious health problems. However, not all are counselled in this way, for this command was given to Timothy on account of his physical ailments, in particular, it seems, those of his digestive system.

The concluding two verses warn against a premature assessment of the character and conduct of men generally, but in this context particularly of those who aspire to be elders. The sinful deeds of some may be *conspicuous* and so lead the way to a correct human judgment antedating the Final Judgment; but other sins may be concealed, so that further probing and lengthy enquiry may be necessary to discover them. Those who have sinned against the Lord are warned in Numbers 32:23, 'Be sure your sin will find you out', and he can guide his appointed judges in the church.

In the same way, some good works may be *conspicuous*, while others may be modestly hidden from public view, being done to God's glory and not to gain a reputation inside or outside the church. Yet by means of careful investigation these also can be brought to light and the correct assessment made of the person's fitness for office. Ultimately, when the Lord comes, he 'will bring to light the things now hidden in darkness and will disclose the purposes of the heart. Then each one will receive his commendation from God' (*1 Cor.* 4:5).

18

Slaves Must Honour Their Masters

Let all who are under a yoke as slaves regard their own masters as worthy of all honour, so that the name of God and the teaching may not be reviled. ² Those who have believing masters must not be disrespectful on the ground that they are brothers; rather they must serve all the better since those who benefit by their good service are believers and beloved. Teach and urge these things (1 Tim. 6:1–2).

This brief passage deals with the great problem faced by Christians who were slaves. The descriptive phrase *under a yoke* emphasizes that being a slave could be as galling to the spirit as an actual yoke to the neck and shoulders. Their despotic masters had total authority over them, in the view of the state, and many abused this, with concern only for their own prosperity and none for the slave's welfare. In his earlier letter to this church, Paul had already dealt with the attitude and conduct of Christian slaves when he taught that giving honour to masters involved obedience, even as bondservants of Christ, doing the will of God from the heart (*Eph.* 6:5–8) .

This duty is also required in Colossians 3:22–24. There it is linked with the encouragement that in giving obedient service with sincerity of heart they served the Lord Christ, and would receive the inheritance of his servants. Similar instructions are given in Titus 2:9, 'Slaves are to be submissive to their own masters in everything; they are to be well-pleasing, not argumentative.' However, God does not permit masters absolute dominance over their slaves, for in Ephesians 6:9 and Colossians 4:1 he teaches masters that they have a Master in heaven to whom they must give account, and so they should treat their slaves justly and fairly, without threatening them.

This requirement that slaves should be obedient and honour their masters accords with the general teaching of Romans 13:1,7, 'Let every person be subject to the governing authorities . . . Pay honour to whom honour is owed.' Insubordination would be resistance to what God has appointed, and the Christian slave should be concerned that his conduct does not dishonour God nor bring disgrace to Christian teaching. He ought rather to have the positive aim taught in Titus 2:10, to show all good faith and honesty, so that in everything he does he will adorn the doctrine of God our Saviour.

By the phrase *the name of God* (verse 1), Paul draws attention to God's character as revealed in his Word. *The teaching* therefore is his, and when a Christian's behaviour conflicts with scriptural teaching it reflects badly on the God whom he professes to obey. As the holy name of the LORD was profaned among the nations by the life style of the Jews (*Ezek.* 36:21, *Rom.* 2:24), so professing Christians dishonour God by their disobedience to his commands.

We recognize here the underlying principle that the Christian slave must be primarily concerned for God's honour, rather than selfishly caring about his own comfort or convenience, and this is relevant to every believer whatever his or her status or occupation in life. All Christians should be dominated in their thoughts and motives, not by their personal or general 'human rights', but by a consuming passion to do all for the glory of God.

Some Christian slaves were privileged to have *believing masters*, and this could stir up another kind of problem in that they might be tempted to despise them and refuse to honour them with obedient service. Because they were brethren in Christ, who should love one another, a slave might think that discipline would not be enforced. Therefore he might try his master's patience and forbearance by slackness or surliness. There is, of course, a need for a proper understanding of the implications of Galatians 3:28, 'There is neither slave nor free . . . for you are all one in Christ Jesus.' All are equally precious to the Lord Jesus Christ, but we must recognize that in society roles, gifts, and relationships differ, just as male and female differ.

We observed in 1:10 that the forcible enslaving of men is condemned as 'contrary to sound doctrine', but here we discover also that God does not command Christian masters to release their slaves. These two passages cannot be contrary to one another, for God is all-wise and consistent in his teaching. Therefore we must recognize that, in the situation then prevailing, the action that would be best for their slaves might well be to retain them.

The outward formal distinction recognized by society might well remain, but the fact that master and slave belonged together to Christ and his church would also find expression. This is well illustrated in the case of the counsel given to Philemon regarding Onesimus, an unprofitable slave who had wronged him and absconded, but then become a Christian under Paul's ministry, so that he called him 'my child' and 'my very heart'. 'Have him back', Paul says, ' . . . no longer as a slave but more than a slave, as a beloved brother – specially to me, but how much more to you, both in the flesh and in the Lord' (*Philem.* 15–16).

In verse 2 the relationship of master and slave in God's family is the reason why, instead of despising a Christian master, the believing slave should be concerned to serve him well, in order that he might be benefited by his labour. Interestingly, the verb *serve* denotes the work of a slave; Christians ought to be prepared to 'slave away' for the good of their brethren in Christ, because they are believers and beloved.

Though this teaching relates directly to slaves, we may recognize that it provides good guidance for Christians in their relationships with employers. They should be diligent and hardworking to commend the Christian faith and acknowledge God's ordering of their situation. It must be realized that not all slaves performed what we would call menial tasks, for some would have been teachers, lawyers, and doctors. Therefore the principles of service apply to all.

Timothy is commanded to keep teaching *these things*, which may include all the preceding verses from the commencement of chapter 5, or simply focus on these two verses in chapter 6 because of their importance. This may have been necessary because of the difficulty Christian slaves felt about compliance, but Timothy must continue to urge that they should respond obediently to the apostolic commands.

19

False Teaching and
the Love of Money

If anyone teaches a different doctrine and does not agree with the sound words of our Lord Jesus Christ and the teaching that accords with godliness, ⁴ he is puffed up with conceit, and understands nothing. He has an unhealthy craving for controversy and for quarrels about words, which produce envy, dissension, slander, evil suspicions, ⁵ and constant friction among people who are depraved in mind and deprived of the truth, imagining that godliness is a means of gain. ⁶ Now there is great gain in godliness with contentment, ⁷ for we brought nothing into the world, and we cannot take anything out of the world. ⁸ But if we have food and clothing, with these we will be content. ⁹ But those who desire to be rich fall into temptation, into a snare, into many senseless and harmful desires that plunge people into ruin and destruction. ¹⁰ For the love of money is a root of all kinds of evils. It is through this craving that some have wandered away from the faith and pierced themselves with many pangs (1 Tim. 6:3–10).

Here the apostle returns to the concern he raised in 1:3, where Timothy was solemnly charged to put a stop to teaching which was contrary to the truths of the Christian faith and did not promote godly edifying. The basic, simple test of the content of a person's teaching is, 'Does it agree with apostolic doctrine and the truths revealed in God's Word?' Among the shortcomings of a teacher of a *different doctrine*, Paul lists the fact that he does not give mental assent and commit himself to those *sound words* of biblical doctrine that promote the spiritual health of Christians. These are included in the spiritual diet commended in 1 Peter 2:2, the pure spiritual milk of God's Word, by means of which Christians will grow up to salvation. Sound or healthy doctrine was mentioned in 1:10, and its importance is also urged in 2 Timothy 1:13 and 4:3.

Since, in secular Greek usage, 'healthy' could denote 'trustworthy', we may also recognize that sense here.

The further description of these words as *of our Lord Jesus Christ* deserves fuller comment because of its importance. It indicates and even emphasizes that Christ is the source of wholesome teaching, and the full title emphasizes his deity, his person and his office as the Messianic Saviour. He had taught his apostles, 'If they kept my word, they will also keep yours' (*John* 15:20), so that the apostle John could write in 1 John 4:6, 'We are from God. Whoever knows God listens to us.'

All who quarrel with apostolic teaching and reject its authority must realize that they are opposing the Lord of the church who is its true Author, and are thus setting aside the doctrine that *accords with* and promotes true *godliness*. The great value of godliness has already been considered in 4:7–8. Faithful Christian teaching always has the aim of inculcating the reverent awe of God that is gained under his blessing.

There follows (verses 4–5) a searching critique of the person who teaches otherwise than God's Word permits. We may profitably clarify the details given, which include both moral and intellectual failures.

He is beclouded with pride so that his mind is befuddled, a danger that was warned against in 3:6 as particularly likely in a new convert. This *conceit* is accompanied with failure to understand vital Christian truths.

Such a man is unhealthily obsessed with questionings and discussions instead of proclaiming the truth, and with mere word-battles instead of profitable teaching. These arguments are contentious disputes about words rather than doctrines. A modern example might be found in attempts to distinguish between 'infallible' and 'inerrant' as descriptions of the inspired and completely true Word of God. Disputes of this kind have serious consequences, as they bring divisions within the church, so that there is a failure of that love which is God's design for her life (1:5).

Envy means displeasure or grief at another's good and is well defined in the *Concise Oxford Dictionary* as 'grudging contemplation of more fortunate persons'. This inner resentment finds expression in heated disagreements and often, as in warfare, truth is the first casualty, so that one person makes slanderous allegations against another, defaming his character, to boost his own standing.

Evil suspicions arise in other's minds when a person's words or deeds are improperly reckoned to have wicked or harmful intentions. Hendriksen quotes Pope's acute observation, 'All looks yellow to the jaundiced eye' (*New Testament Commentary: Timothy and Titus*, p. 197).

The result is *constant friction* (verse 5). The NKJV has 'useless wranglings' here, based on a variant to the Majority Greek text. The latter has a rather stronger term meaning 'mutual irritations and persistent altercations'. The term is derived from the abrasive rubbing of objects together.

Such behaviour is the characteristic of those who are in a seriously flawed mental, moral and spiritual condition. The *mind* here includes according to Ellicott, 'the willing and the thinking part in man', and when that is corrupted or *depraved*, conscience does not function as it ought, so that truth is opposed and falsehood espoused. When a man is *deprived of the truth*, it is implied that, having dismissed it, like those in Titus 1:14 ('who turn away from the truth'), the truth is then taken away from him.

One element in the perverted thinking of such men, is their false supposition that *godliness is a means of* procuring *gain*, for they are motivated by covetousness. This attitude was critically exposed by Peter in Acts 8:18–20, when Simon offered him money in return for the power to impart the Holy Spirit by the laying on of his hands. The selling of pardons and other church privileges – widespread in the pre-Reformation church – is named 'simony', after this incident, but the same fault is prevalent in all cults and sects where leaders offer spiritual or material blessings in return for monetary gifts.

One characteristic of false teachers is referred to in 2 Peter 2:3,15, 'In their greed they will exploit you with false words . . . They have followed the way of Balaam, the son of Beor, who loved gain from wrongdoing.' We should note that the silversmiths in Ephesus made great financial profit by manufacturing and selling images of the goddess Artemis at Ephesus (*Acts* 19:24), and such enrichment from false religions and perversions of Christianity has been common through the centuries. When Paul had met with the elders from Ephesus he claimed, 'I coveted no one's silver or gold or apparel. You yourselves know that these hands ministered to my necessities' (*Acts* 20:33–34), and he wrote in 1 Thessalonians 2:5, 'We never came with words of flattery, as you know, nor with a pretext for greed—God is witness.' The fault here exposed was found in Crete where empty talkers and deceivers were 'teaching for shameful gain what they ought not to teach'. 'They must be silenced', Paul insists (*Titus* 1:10–11).

The command closing verse 5 in some versions, 'From such withdraw yourself', is omitted by the ESV because it is absent from early Greek manuscripts, though it is excellent advice, and is supported by early versions and some patristic testimony.

Having criticized the wrong conception in verse 5, Paul proceeds to teach that *godliness* is truly *great gain* when accompanied with *contentment* (verse 6). This develops his statement in 4:8, 'Godliness is of value in every way.' Though he had experienced deprivation and been abased, he wrote in Philippians 4:11, 'I have learned in whatever situation I am to be content.' This contentment is totally different from self-sufficiency. It is, rather, full satisfaction with the Lord Jesus Christ as his all-sufficient Saviour and Lord, who strengthens him and gives him competence for the exercise of his ministry.

Paul has no concern about earthly riches but, having been made rich through Christ's poverty (*2 Cor.* 8:9), is content with treasure in heaven. There is, of course, also great present gain in the enjoyment of Christ's rich provision for the daily lives of his own family of believers. They can affirm with David, 'The LORD is my shepherd', and add, 'I shall not want' (*Psa.* 23:1). So in 1 Chronicles 29:12 David blessed the Lord and declared, 'Both riches and honour come from you, and you rule over all.' It is this assurance that enables the Christian to be content with the bare necessities of life, for God his Father in heaven knows what is best and always acts in love, whether he gives or withholds.

It is an observable and obvious fact that no one is able to *take anything out of the world* (verse 7) when he dies. Though it may also have been a contemporary proverbial saying, this truth was revealed in the Scriptures. Job acknowledged it in the context of his bereavement (*Job* 1:21), 'Naked I came from my mother's womb, and naked shall I return', and, with general reference to the rich, Solomon comments, '[He] shall take nothing for his toil that he may carry away in his hand' (*Eccles.* 5:15). Lamentations 3:24–25 records a positive affirmation of a believer at a time of great affliction and bewilderment that reveals contentment: 'The LORD is my portion, says my soul, therefore I will hope in him. The LORD is good to those who wait for him, to the soul who seeks him.'

The Lord Jesus taught his disciples that they should not worry about food and clothing because God, their heavenly Father, knows they need these things. They ought instead to seek first his kingdom and righteousness (*Matt.* 6:31–33). The word translated 'clothing', though used by Josephus, a contemporary Jewish writer, with the more restricted meaning, can also include shelter and indicate the value of having a home. The apostle had taught believers at Corinth that, since they belonged to Christ, 'all things are yours' (*1 Cor.* 3:21). Therefore they should surely be content with the minimum of temporal possessions. Not only is Christian contentment enjoyed without earthly riches, the pursuit of riches will actually bring dissatisfaction, for as Solomon commented in Ecclesiastes 5:10, 'He who loves money will not be satisfied with money, nor he who loves wealth with his income; this also is vanity.'

To *desire to be rich* (verse 9) involves the deliberate exercise of a man's will. It is not a passing impulse that is meant but a settled purpose of mind to become and remain wealthy, and those with this determination *fall into temptation* which, like a *snare*, entangles its victim, making it very hard to get free. We must note that Paul does not teach that it is a mere possibility but a fact: they *do* fall. Therefore no one should assume that he will be an exception. He must take heed to himself.

This *snare,* set by the devil, brings a person into the sphere of strong *desires* that are *senseless*, or unreasonable, in that they have not been carefully thought about and bring great harm. The serious nature of these hurtful lusts is that, whatever temporal benefit is gained, they bring irretrievable loss, for they drown men in *ruin and destruction.* The combination of these two nouns emphasizes the ruinous end of this way of life for the whole man, both body and spirit; it is destructive of the personality and brings eternal punishment under the wrath of almighty God.

[105]

The love of money is clearly a breach of the commandment, 'You shall not covet' (*Exod.* 20:17). It was a fault of the Pharisees (*Luke* 16:14) and of some scribes, 'who devour widows' houses and for a pretence make long prayers' (*Mark* 12:40). Paul describes covetousness as idolatry in Colossians 3:5, revealing the danger that money may be put in the place that God alone should have in our affections and devotion.

The ESV translation clarifies the sense of verse 10; the love of money is not so much 'the root of all evil', a questionable statement, but *a root of all kinds of evils.* Those who reach out with the arms of their hearts to embrace wealth are deceived and are led far astray from the pathway illumined by Scripture, along which believers walk (*Psa.* 119:105). In pursuing this course of life they inflict upon themselves great pain, like that known in the physical realm when the body is badly scratched by thorns or *pierced* by spears, and here called *many pangs.* These pangs are described using a word related to that used by the rich man in the parable of the Lord Jesus in Luke 16, verses 24–25. He was 'in anguish' under divine wrath and described his condition as being in a 'place of torment' (*Luke* 16:28). The sorrows in question would include remorseful disillusionment, and such 'frightful torments of conscience', as Calvin calls them, as may be experienced before death. E. K. Simpson remarked on one aspect of this: 'Many a millionaire, after choking his soul with gold-dust, has died from melancholia.' William Hendriksen provides an illustration from the suicide letter of a very wealthy man: 'When I was an ordinary workman in New York, I was happy. Now that I possess millions I am infinitely sad and prefer death' (*New Testament Commentary: Timothy and Titus*, p. 201).

20

The Charge to Timothy
concerning His Ministry

But as for you, O man of God, flee these things. Pursue righteousness, godliness, faith, love, steadfastness, gentleness. [12] Fight the good fight of the faith. Take hold of the eternal life to which you were called and about which you made the good confession in the presence of many witnesses. [13] I charge you in the presence of God, who gives life to all things, and of Christ Jesus, who in his testimony before Pontius Pilate made the good confession, [14] to keep the commandment unstained and free from reproach until the appearing of our Lord Jesus Christ, [15] which he will display at the proper time—he who is the blessed and only Sovereign, the King of kings and Lord of lords, [16] who alone has immortality, who dwells in unapproachable light, whom no one has ever seen or can see. To him be honour and eternal dominion. Amen (1 Tim. 6:11–16).

After the description of some false teachers who are destitute of the truth and suppose that godliness is a means of gain, the apostle turns to Timothy with this solemn charge, introduced by the emphatic, 'O man of God'. This descriptive phrase was surely designed to remind him that he belonged to God and had been entrusted by him with the privileged task of overseeing the life of the church at Ephesus. The term 'man of God' was used of Moses (*Deut.* 33:1), and of many prophets, and the widow's word to Elijah, 'I know that you are a man of God, and that the word of the LORD in your mouth is truth' (*1 Kings* 17:24), would serve as a guide to Timothy in his responsibility. This means that he must *flee* from those things criticized in verses 3–10, keeping as far away from them as possible because they are unworthy of a servant of God, but must also *pursue* or follow closely the standard of life that is here commended.

'The LORD is righteous; he loves righteous deeds' (*Psa.* 11:7), and 'he loves him who pursues righteousness' (*Prov.* 15:9), as Timothy is here urged to do. This is akin to hungering and thirsting for righteousness (*Matt.* 5:6), and requires the conforming of Timothy's dispositions and behaviour to the standards revealed in God's Word, after the pattern of Psalm 119:106, 'I have sworn an oath and confirmed it, to keep your righteous rules.' Such conduct is related in 1 Peter 2:24 to the purpose of Christ's atoning death on the cross, that those whose sins he bore should live to righteousness, and in Romans 6:18 it is said that believers, having been set free from sin, have become slaves of righteousness.

The importance of *godliness* in the life of the Christian has already been stressed in 2:1,10 and 6:6, and Timothy himself was urged, 'Train yourself for godliness' (4:7). This reverent devotion to God should be a dominant characteristic of Timothy's personal life, as he brings 'holiness to completion in the fear of God' (*2 Cor.* 7:1). The Hebrew expression 'the fear of the LORD' is often translated in the LXX as 'godliness'. It should also pervade Timothy's ministry, so that it conforms to the pattern God commended in his service: 'He [Levi] feared me, and was reverent before my name' (*Mal.* 2:5, my preferred translation).

Faith here almost certainly must denote the ongoing exercise of faith and trust in God and his promises that is of the essence of the Christian life, just as Paul wrote, 'I live by faith in the Son of God, who loved me and gave himself for me' (*Gal.* 2:20).

Timothy was instructed in 4:12 to be an example to other believers in both *faith* and *love*, and these supreme Christian graces are conjoined again in the exhortation of 2 Timothy 2:22. He had earlier observed and reported to Paul the good news of the faith and love of the Christians in Thessalonica (*1 Thess.* 3:6) which were an evidence of their conversion (*1 Thess.* 1:3–4), and an example to others.

Steadfastness is the patient endurance exercised in bearing up bravely under tribulations and hostile pressures. God himself is called 'the God of endurance', or steadfastness (*Rom.* 15:5), and Timothy had seen this quality exemplified in Paul (*2 Tim.* 3:10).

The Greek noun translated here *gentleness,* and found nowhere else in the New Testament, is explained by Ellicott as a reference to meekness of heart or feelings, for it is a compound of the adjective 'meek', and so may be considered as the virtue exhibited by the Lord Jesus who was 'gentle [or meek] and lowly in heart' (*Matt.* 11:29; see also *2 Cor.* 10:1).

Earlier, in 1:18, Timothy's charge was expressed using a military metaphor; he was to be engaged in warfare as a soldier. Here (verse 12) the terminology is changed: he is continually to engage in the *good* (or excellent) *fight* on the Lord's behalf, to promote the Christian faith. It is perhaps significant that in 2 Timothy 4:6 Paul uses the same terminology. We could translate his words, 'The good contest I have contested.' The English verb 'agonize' is a transliteration of the Greek verb. The same verb was used by Paul in 1 Corinthians 9:25 of the action of one who contends for a prize by exercising self-control in all things, and the same strict self-discipline is necessary in the Christian life and the Christian ministry.

It is in the context of this continual struggle that Timothy will once for all lay firm *hold* on *eternal life*. Though already possessed by every believer, the consummation of eternal life awaits the coming glorious day of resurrection. Christians are encouraged by James 1:12, 'Blessed is the man who remains steadfast under trial, for when he has stood the test he will receive the crown of life, which God has promised to those who love him', and by the Lord Jesus in Revelation 2:10, 'Be faithful unto death, and I will give you the crown of life.'

Timothy is next reminded that he was effectually *called* by God into eternal life by means of the gospel. This happened, as 2 Timothy 1:9 teaches, 'because of [God's] own purpose and grace'. He then *made the good confession* before *many witnesses*. The link with God's call suggests that this occurred shortly after his conversion, perhaps at his baptism, when he publicly professed his faith in the Lord Jesus Christ as his Saviour, according to Romans 10:9. 'If you confess with your mouth that Jesus is Lord and believe in your heart that God raised him from the dead, you will be saved.' John Calvin, however, prefers to regard it as the faithful confession Timothy made throughout his previous ministry: 'You have many witnesses of your illustrious confession who have beheld you acting faithfully and sincerely in the profession of the gospel.'

The charge given in the preceding two verses is further solemnized in verse 13 as Paul sets it in the context of God's all-seeing eye (*in the presence of God*), a fact that would inspire Timothy with awe, while also encouraging him to expect divine assistance and protection in his ministry.

This is enhanced by the description of God as the one who *gives life to all things*. Most manuscripts have the more usual verb for 'make alive' here, while others have a verb which means 'preserve alive', and is used of the midwives' action in Exodus 1:17 (LXX), and Acts 7:19. Since God both endues with life and sustains it, Timothy and every Christian may be encouraged to rely on him to enliven them throughout their lives.

Timothy is further taught that his charge is given in the presence of Christ Jesus, who himself *made the good confession,* for he bore clear witness to his Person as God's Son and his office as Saviour, though that brought on him the animosity of the Jewish leaders and led to his sufferings, crucifixion and death. Paul was clearly aware of those events, whether from eyewitnesses or the Gospel record (see note on 5:18 for Paul's attitude to Luke's Gospel). The preposition 'before' in the phrase *before Pontius Pilate* may well denote 'in the time of'. Jesus is the faithful and true witness (*Rev.* 1:5; 3:14), and in the presence of Pilate he explained that he was a king and had come to bear witness to the truth (*John* 18:37). Since the Lord Jesus is exalted as a trustworthy and sympathetic Saviour, Christians should be greatly encouraged as his witnesses and expect the enabling power of the Holy Spirit.

The *commandment* that Timothy is required to keep (verse 14) most naturally refers to the preceding verses, though the whole of the epistle provides more details of its contents. In the discharge of this ministry he must aim to be *unstained*, that is, without blemish on his character, and also without bringing *reproach* on himself, that is, positively deserving of good report. The first adjective is used in James 1:27, where religion that is pure and undefiled before God is shown to include keeping oneself unstained from the world; and Christians are urged in 2 Peter 3:14 to give diligence to be found without spot, or unstained, in the day of the Lord.

We have already noted the other phrase, *free from reproach*, in connection with the divine requirements for elders (3:2, there translated 'above reproach'), and in connection with the widows who deserve the financial support of the church (5:7, there translated 'without reproach').

In the discharge of this task Timothy can look forward to *the appearing of our Lord Jesus Christ*, when he comes with glory and power at the consummation of history (*2 Thess.* 2:8). The noun is used in the LXX of a display of divine glory, and by Paul again in 2 Timothy 1:10; 4:1,8, and Titus 2:13 where it is amplified, 'the appearing of the glory of our great God and Saviour Jesus Christ'.

God has appointed his own *proper time* for this wondrous *display* (verse 15) and has been pleased to keep its timing a mystery, though he requires men to be ready and prepared, just as Jesus said, 'You also must be ready, for the Son of Man is coming at an hour you do not expect' (*Matt.* 24:44).

There follows an ascription of praise and glory to God the Father. It begins by describing him as *the blessed and only Sovereign*, who will give this display. Earlier, in 1:11, Paul described God as 'blessed' in relation to the gospel, but here emphasis falls on his supreme sovereignty. Ellicott has a fine note on this: 'Blessed indeed is God, not only on account of his own immutable and essential perfections, but also on account of the riches of his mercy.'

He is the *only Sovereign.* 'Potentate' (AV, NKJV, ASV) well translates the original Greek term, for it emphasizes the possession of total power, as in Psalm 62:11, 'Power belongs to God.' This power was exercised in creation – 'It is he who made the earth by his power' (*Jer.* 10:12) – and it is to be recognized both in providence and in redemption, so that God's people are encouraged to praise him for it. He is the Almighty God whose purposes none can delay or thwart and he will bring human history to its consummation at this *appearing of our Lord Jesus Christ.* As in the beginning God created the heavens and the earth, so in the day of the Lord he will act to purge the earth by fire and refashion it, as he has promised, to provide new heavens and a new earth in which righteousness dwells (*2 Pet.* 3:10–13).

God's power is already, and always, being exercised even over all earthly kings and lords. He reigns over all who reign and lords it over all who lord it over others. All the governments of the world are subject to his dominion (*Dan.* 4:34–35), and, 'The king's heart is a stream of water in the hand of the LORD; he turns it wherever he will' (*Prov.* 21:1).

The title *Lord of lords* is ascribed to the LORD in Deuteronomy 10:17 and Psalm 136:3, and in Revelation 17:14 the triumph of the Lamb is attributed to the fact that 'he is Lord of lords and King of kings.'

God *alone has immortality* (verse 16). It belongs to his essential nature and he uniquely enjoys it. He is not only undying and deathless, but also the fountain of life to all living creatures. At the coming of the Lord Jesus Christ, believers are assured that their resurrection to life means that 'this mortal body must put on immortality', and so God's promise will be fulfilled, 'Death is swallowed up in victory' (*1 Cor.* 15:53–54). Just as God is immortal, or imperishable (1:17), so the Christian dead shall be raised imperishable, for they shall all be changed and made free from all corruption.

Because God *dwells* in *light*, a symbol of his glorious majesty, no created being can approach him, a truth which is celebrated in Psalm 104:1–2, 'O LORD my God, you are very great! You are clothed with splendour and majesty, covering yourself with light as with a garment.' This solemn fact recalls the occasion when God manifested his glory on Mount Sinai and forbad the Israelites to approach on pain of death, and the time when he said to Moses in Exodus 33:20, 'You cannot see my face, for man shall not see me and live.'

Paul enlarges on the truth that God is invisible, mentioned in 1:17, by explaining that *no one has ever seen* God *or can see* him. We have no natural power in our eyes to behold him, and no intellectual faculty to comprehend him or understand all his ways.

The main response that these profound truths draw from the believer is that of adoring praise. To him belong, as an inalienable right, both *honour and eternal dominion.* 'Ascribe to the LORD the glory due his name; worship the LORD in the splendour of holiness' (*Psa.* 29:2). 'Worthy are you, our Lord and God, to receive glory and honour and power, for you created all things, and by your will they existed and were created' (*Rev.* 4:11).

Two Closing Commands to Timothy

As for the rich in this present age, charge them not to be haughty, nor to set their hopes on the uncertainty of riches, but on God, who richly provides us with everything to enjoy. [18] They are to do good, to be rich in good works, to be generous and ready to share, [19] thus storing up treasure for themselves as a good foundation for the future, so that they may take hold of that which is truly life.

[20] O Timothy, guard the deposit entrusted to you. Avoid the irreverent babble and contradictions of what is falsely called 'knowledge', [21] for by professing it some have swerved from the faith. Grace be with you (1 Tim. 6:17–21).

Paul has already given commands regarding the love of money, because of the danger that it leads some to stray from the faith (verses 9–10), and has instructed Timothy regarding the need for diligence in his Christian life and ministry (verses 11–14). Now, as he brings the letter to its close, he returns to these important matters.

Firstly (verses 17–19), he deals directly with those who have money, describing them as *rich in this present age*, a phrase that immediately reminds them of the severe limitations of earthly wealth: it cannot be permanently possessed, and its owners will be parted from it at death, if not before.

The rich are warned, through Timothy, against being *haughty* (verse 17), or feeling that they are superior to the poor, for such arrogance is totally unwarranted and is contrary to the basic Christian virtue of humility: 'Clothe yourselves, all of you, with humility towards one another, for God opposes the proud' (*1 Pet.* 5:5).

If they have *set their hopes on the uncertainty of riches* they are utterly at fault, for the word-order in the original emphasizes the fact that riches do not and cannot offer anything fixed and secure for their owners. Proverbs 23:4–5 provides good counsel: 'Do not toil to acquire wealth; be discerning enough to desist. When your eyes light on it, it is gone, for suddenly it sprouts wings, flying like an eagle towards heaven.' Financial investments may lose their value, expensive purchases may be stolen or deteriorate, and when the rich die they lose everything! The rich man must learn not to boast in his riches, but in his knowledge of the Lord, who practises steadfast love, justice, and righteousness in the earth (*Jer.* 9:23–24).

Then, more directly, the rich man is urged to set his hope firmly and exclusively in God who, in his sovereign rule in providence, *richly provides us with everything to enjoy.* He is the giver of every good and perfect gift, and bears witness to this in the provision of rain and fruitful seasons (*Acts* 14:17, *Psa.* 104:14–15). Though many early Greek manuscripts do not include the adjective 'living' as descriptive of God in verse 17, its prior use in 3:15, and 4:10 would certainly justify recognizing its relevance here, in contrast with rich men, who must die. It is vital to acknowledge that whatever riches men have are due to God's generous giving and therefore they must regard them as held in trust from him, to whom they must give account for the use of them.

In verses 17 and 18, the rich are warned against two dangers: a proud independence that does not acknowledge God's goodness, and a self-importance that blinds them to the needs of the poor. Christians should appreciate the good things that they have to make their life on earth pleasant, so that they praise God for them, but their joy should not degenerate into self-indulgence in pleasurable activities.

As the original Greek noun for *riches* includes the meaning of the advantage derived from possessing them, we can recognize and press that sense here, for the advantage the Christian rich have is the ability to do good with their wealth, as God has commanded. They must aim to be rich towards God, and instead of overvaluing the possession of earthly riches they should use them for the good of others: 'Blessed is the one who considers the poor' (*Psa.* 41:1). It is surely worthy of note that the apostle Paul had shared with the elders at Ephesus the relevant words of the Lord Jesus,

'It is more blessed to give than to receive' (*Acts* 20:35). In his parable of the farmer who, after a good harvest, boasted of the future (*Luke* 12:15–21), Jesus himself warned that putting confidence in acquired riches is utter folly that will be exposed in the day of judgment, and he applied the parable in this way: 'So is the one who lays up treasure for himself and is not rich towards God.'

The command to be *generous and ready to share* employs two adjectives that are found nowhere else in the New Testament. The first indicates that the rich should delight in giving and do so freely; the second suggests that this is a vital ingredient in Christian fellowship, as the expression of genuine loving concern. Hebrews 13:16 conveys the same idea, 'Do not neglect to do good and to share what you have, for such sacrifices are pleasing to God.' In Galatians 6:10, Christians are taught the same responsibility, 'So then, as we have opportunity, let us do good to everyone, and especially to those who are of the household of faith.'

Verse 19 provides another dimension to Christian giving by revealing that it *stores up treasure* in heaven that is an excellent *foundation for the future*. The Lord Jesus gave this advice, 'Lay up for yourselves treasures in heaven' (*Matt.* 6:20), and he also taught the rich young ruler, 'Sell what you possess and give to the poor, and you will have treasure in heaven; and come, follow me' (*Matt.* 19:21).

This wise counsel should be contrasted with the solemn warning given to the rich in James 5:1–6 that hoarding wealth improperly will bring down God's judgment on them. Christians must always live in the light of the future, for they have been born again to a living hope and to an inheritance that is kept in heaven for them (*1 Pet.* 1:3–4).

The parable of the unjust steward in Luke 16 touches on this theme, for he acted prudently though unjustly in making provision for his future, and such wise and faithful use of one's money in the light of eternity is commended by Jesus: 'Make friends for yourselves by means of unrighteous wealth, so that when it fails they may receive you into the eternal dwellings' (*Luke* 16:9).

We are further taught that such a characteristic lifestyle and course of action in generous giving is the means whereby the believer takes firm hold on the life that has eternal value.

Secondly (verses 20–21), we find an impassioned, urgent charge to Timothy. The fact that he is appealed to by name would surely impress it indelibly on his mind and heart. A *deposit* is something that is entrusted to a person for him to keep safe. This is illustrated in Leviticus 6:2, 4 (LXX). In 2 Timothy 1:14 there is an enlargement of this charge: 'By the Holy Spirit who dwells within us, guard the good deposit entrusted to you.' Timothy must guard and protect 'the faith that was once for all delivered to the saints' (*Jude* 3) from attacks on its truth, by positive preaching that expounds it and by refuting those who contradict it.

This task involves avoiding the nonsense, even gibberish, that is popular among unbelievers whose *babble* is also *irreverent* or profane, in direct opposition to godly truth, for, as explained in 2 Timothy 2:16, 'It will lead people into more and more ungodliness.' John Calvin aptly described this as 'the high-sounding verbose and bombastic style of those who, not content with the simplicity of the gospel, turn it into profane philosophy'. This is similar to the futile verbiage the apostle countered in 1:6–7, where he showed that those who engaged in it had swerved away from God's requirement.

The other problem comes from the direct opposition to the Christian faith, as revealed in the Scriptures, of *what is falsely called knowledge*. The Greek word for 'falsely called' is the basis of our English word 'pseudonymous'. It is probable that Paul was criticizing the early development of the heretical group called the 'Gnostics', though it was in the next century that their harmful influence became more widespread. The Gnostics claimed special knowledge about God and humanity's relationship with him on the basis of their own visions and philosophical enquiries.

Teachers who make claims to superior knowledge deliberately repudiate the uniqueness and sufficiency of biblical revelation. They are usually highly regarded by the unbelieving world. In the nineteenth and twentieth centuries, many such teachers were accepted as scholars and profound thinkers. They affirmed that their ideas and theories were based on what they termed the 'assured results' of scientific or philosophical enquiry.

When men reject the authority of God's Word, it is difficult if not impossible to find a common basis for satisfactory discussion with them. On a topic like creation, for example, Christians neces-sarily start from the biblical conviction that 'in the beginning God created the heavens and the earth' (*Gen.* 1:1). This is an essential foundation of faith, as indicated in Hebrews 11:3, 'By faith we un-derstand that the universe was created by the Word of God.'

The viewpoint of the apostle Paul, writing under the direction of the Holy Spirit, is based on the conviction that the fear of the Lord is the beginning of knowledge (*Prov.* 1:7), and that those who have no fear of God are fools in his sight (*Psa.* 14:1). In 1 Corin-thians 3:18–20, Paul had emphasized that the wisdom of this world is foolishness with God, and it is surely great folly to reject the wisdom of the omniscient God in favour of the opinions of sinful and fallible men.

We give thanks to God for enabling scientists to make discover-ies that have contributed so much that is valuable for our earthly lives, and we recognize that, in their own realms, they do possess valuable knowledge and skill, but when they intrude into the realm of divine truth they lose their credibility and authority. Especially in the last two centuries, opposition to divinely-revealed truth has greatly increased. Its teachers have become more and more arro-gant, so that many Christians often feel unable to affirm the dis-tinctive teaching of Scripture.

There is a solemn warning here that some who have been overly impressed by unscriptural teaching and adopted it as their own profession have *swerved from the faith*, that is, from sound doc-trine. What happened then is sadly happening today: many turn aside from the way of godliness because they seek acceptance in the realms of the 'scholarly intelligentsia', and they are unwilling to be thought fools for Christ's sake. The maintenance of opinions that are in conflict with God's revelation will inevitably mar fel-lowship with him and, since the believer's greatest concern is to walk humbly with God, he must take careful heed to the apostolic admonition.

There is the briefest closing greeting – *Grace be with you* – but we must note that the 'you' is plural in many old manuscripts, so that clearly the apostle anticipated that the letter would be read to or by others. It is an encouragement that, in obedience to all the commands given by God, Timothy may expect and rely on the

sufficiency of the grace of God, as was intimated in 1:2. The closing *Amen* (in the majority of Greek manuscripts, though not in
some of the oldest) may well serve to emphasize that this is certain:
assuredly, this is true.

Group Study Guide

SCHEME FOR GROUP BIBLE STUDY
(Covers 13 weeks. Before each study read the passage indicated and the chapters from this book shown below.)

Study Passage	Chapters
1. 1 Timothy 1:1–11	1–3
2. 1 Timothy 1:12–20	4–5
3. 1 Timothy 2:1–7	6
4. 1 Timothy 2:8–15	7–8
5. 1 Timothy 3:1–7	9
6. 1 Timothy 3:8–13	10
7. 1 Timothy 3:14–16	11
8. 1 Timothy 4:1–10	12–13
9. 1 Timothy 4:11–16	14
10. 1 Timothy 5:1–16	15–16
11. 1 Timothy 5:17–25	17
12. 1 Timothy 6:1–10	18–19
13. 1 Timothy 6:11–21	20–21

This Study Guide has been prepared for group Bible study, but it can also be used individually. Those who use it on their own may find it helpful to keep a note of their responses in a notebook.

The way in which group Bible studies are led can greatly enhance their value. A well-conducted study will appear as though it has been easy to lead, but that is usually because the leader has worked hard and planned well. Clear aims are essential.

LET'S STUDY 1 TIMOTHY

AIMS

In all Bible study, individual or corporate, we have several aims:

1. To gain an understanding of the original meaning of the particular passage of Scripture;

2. To apply this to ourselves and our own situation;

3. To develop some specific ways of putting the biblical teaching into practice.

2 Timothy 3:16–17 provides a helpful structure. Paul says that Scripture is useful for:

i. teaching us;

ii. rebuking us;

iii. correcting, or changing us;

iv. training us in righteousness.

Consequently, in studying any passage of Scripture, we should always have in mind these questions:

What does this passage teach us (about God, ourselves, etc.)?

Does it rebuke us in some way?

How can its teaching transform us?

What equipment does it give us for serving Christ?

In fact, these four questions alone would provide a safe guide in any Bible study.

PRINCIPLES

In group Bible study we meet in order to learn about God's Word and ways 'with all the saints' (*Eph.* 3:18). But our own experience, as well as Scripture, tells us that the saints are not always what they are called to be in every situation – including group Bible study! Leaders ordinarily have to work hard and prepare well if the work of the group is to be spiritually profitable. The following guidelines for leaders may help to make this a reality.

Preparation:

1. Study and understand the passage yourself. The better prepared and more sure of the direction of the study you are, the more likely it is that the group will have a beneficial and enjoyable study. Ask: What are the main things this passage is saying? How can this be made clear? This is not the same question as the more common, 'What does this passage "say to you"?', which expects a reaction rather than an exposition of the passage. Be clear about that distinction yourself, and work at making it clear in the group study.

2. On the basis of your own study form a clear idea *before* the group meets of (i) the main theme(s) of the passage which should be opened out for discussion, and (ii) some general conclusions the group ought to reach as a result of the study. Here the questions which arise from 2 Timothy 3:16–17 should act as our guide.

3. The guidelines and questions which follow may help to provide a general framework for each discussion; leaders should use them as starting places which can be further developed. It is usually helpful to have a specific goal or theme in mind for group discussion, and one is suggested for each study. But even more important than tracing a single theme is understanding the teaching and the implications of the passage.

Leading the Group:

1. Announce the passage and theme for the study, and begin with prayer. In group studies it may be helpful to invite a different person to lead in prayer each time you meet.

2. Introduce the passage and theme, briefly reminding people of its outline and highlighting the content of each subsidiary section.

3. Lead the group through the discussion questions. Use your own if you are comfortable in doing so; those provided may be used, developing them with your own points. As discussion proceeds, continue to encourage the group first of all to discuss the significance of the passage (teaching) and only then its application (meaning for us). It may be helpful to write important points and applications on a board by way of summary as well as visual aid.

[121]

4. At the end of each meeting, remind members of the group of their assignments for the next meeting, and encourage them to come prepared. Be sufficiently prepared as the leader to give specific assignments to individuals, or even couples or groups, to come with specific contributions.

5. Remember that you are the leader of the group! Encourage clear contributions, and do not be embarrassed to ask someone to explain what they have said more fully or to help them to do so ('Do you mean . . . ?').

Most groups include the 'over-talkative', the 'over-silent' and the 'red-herring raisers'! Leaders must control the first, encourage the second and redirect the third! Each leader will develop his or her own most natural way of doing that; but it will be helpful to think out what that is before the occasion arises! The first two groups can be helped by some judicious direction of questions to specific individuals or even groups (for example, 'Jane, you know something about this from personal experience . . .'); the third by redirecting the discussion to the passage itself ('That is an interesting point, but isn't it true that this passage really concentrates on . . . ?'). It may be helpful to break the group up into smaller groups sometimes, giving each subgroup specific points to discuss and to report back on. A wise arranging of these smaller groups may also help each member to participate.

More important than any techniques we may develop is the help of the Spirit enabling us to understand and to apply the Scriptures. Have and encourage a humble, prayerful spirit.

6. Keep faith with the schedule; it is better that some of the group wished the study could have been longer than that others are inconvenienced by it stretching beyond the time limits set.

7. Close in prayer. As time permits, spend the closing minutes in corporate prayer, encouraging the group to apply what they have learned in praise and thanks, intercession and petition.

Group Study Guide

STUDY 1: 1 Timothy 1:1–11

1. Consider the authority that the apostle claims, and the implication that to dismiss or disobey Paul's writings is to reject the rule of Christ himself over his church.

2. How is it possible to obey the command to exercise love without becoming vague about doctrines that causes division, and to maintain sound doctrine without becoming coldly orthodox?

3. Trace the biographical material provided about Timothy's childhood and his early instruction in the holy Scriptures. Does this encourage parents to teach God's Word to children in the early years of their lives (see Proverbs 22:6)?

4. What place is there for the Ten Commandments in the preaching of 'the glorious gospel of the blessed God' and in the living of the Christian life today?

5. Since God's law exposes sexual immorality as sinful, how should we respond to legislation that condones it and requires Christians to conform? How can we apply the apostles' insistence, 'We must obey God rather than men' (*Acts* 5:29), as we aim to convict such sinners and bring them to repentance and faith?

FOR STUDY 2: Read 1 Timothy 1:12–20, and chapters 4–5.

STUDY 2: 1 Timothy 1:12–20

1. Consider Paul's experience of mercy in the light of his former way of life, and how it is a pattern to others of Christ's longsuffering. Has verse 15 helped you to find peace with God? To what extent do you share Thomas Bilney's regard for that verse as 'the most sweet and comfortable sentence to my soul'?

2. How in Christian experience does the overflowing of the grace of our Lord relate to the faith and love that are in Christ Jesus? How significant is it that faith is put first?

3. In his ascription of honour and glory to God, Paul concentrates on the attributes of God, rather than focusing only on his experience of saving grace. What lessons should we learn from this for our personal and congregational praise of God?

4. What is involved in 'waging the good warfare', and how vital are faith and a good conscience in preserving the Christian from shipwreck?

5. How important is church discipline for the life of the church and each of its members, in its general application and in excommunication? How, and why, must all be involved if it is to achieve its major aims? (See also 1 Corinthians 5:4, 11.)

FOR STUDY 3: Read 1 Timothy 2:1–7, and chapter 6.

STUDY 3: 1 Timothy 2:1–7

1. What do you think about the priority given here to the prayer life of the church, and the aspects of prayer that Paul mentions? Are these things adequately reflected in your congregation and your own devotions?

2. How should we show our gratitude to God, when we live in an orderly and stable society, knowing that many fellow Christians suffer under hostile regimes?

3. Being saved means coming to the knowledge of the truth (verse 4). Given God's willingness to save, what are our responsibilities to share the truth, and how can we best actually discharge them?

4. Consider the fitness of Christ Jesus to be the one Mediator between God and man and the means by which he fulfils this office (note also Acts 5:31).

5. When might it be necessary for Christians to insist, even on oath, that they are speaking the truth, in order to defend their integrity and commend the gospel of Christ (see verse 7)?

FOR STUDY 4: Read 1 Timothy 2:8–15, and chapters 7–8

STUDY 4: 1 Timothy 2:8–15

1. Though only the man actually praying is directly required to be 'without anger or quarrelling', does this not imply that all who engage with him in congregational worship ought to be like him in their inner disposition?

2. How could the wearing of costly clothing and expensive jewellery, by men or women, adversely affect them and others when they share in congregational worship, even though God looks on the heart?

3. Does the command that Christian women should learn quietly have positive value as a recognition that they are not intellectually inferior to men but ought to exercise their minds as fully as possible, especially in the realm of Christian truth?

4. What is the relevance of 1 Corinthians 11:3 in assessing the divine requirement of women's submission to men in marriage and in church order?

5. Do you agree that verse 15 refers to the child-bearing of Mary? If so, does Paul's emphasis on the need to continue in faith, love, and holiness, with self control, apply to men as well as women?

FOR STUDY 5: Read 1 Timothy 3:1–7, and chapter 9.

STUDY 5: 1 Timothy 3:1–7

1. If a man claims to have a divine call to become an elder or overseer, how can a congregation test that call, without questioning his integrity and his standing as a Christian?

2. What kind of training for the work of overseeing the church do you think is most appropriate? If a candidate for eldership has successfully completed a suitable academic course, what extra factor should a congregation look for in considering him?

3. Since the quality of the life of a prospective elder must be assessed to find out if he meets the scriptural standards, how can this be done without intruding into his privacy or questioning his wife and family?

4. Consider the warnings about giving the authority and the responsibility of the work of an elder to a newly-converted man. Are there any exceptions to this rule?

FOR STUDY 6: Read 1 Timothy 3:8–13 and chapter 10.

STUDY 6: 1 Timothy 3:8–13

1. In this and related passages, is the work of a deacon distinguished from that of an elder? How should this distinction be maintained in churches today? Is it in your congregation?

2. Why should deacons need to 'hold the mystery of the faith with a clear conscience' when their own task does not include teaching in the church?

3. How valuable are the qualifications given in verse 11 to any Christian woman who seeks to serve the Lord in ways that are not recognized as a scriptural office?

FOR STUDY 7: Read 1 Timothy 3:14–16 and chapter 11.

STUDY 7: 1 Timothy 3:14–16

1. How does the glorious nature of the church revealed here serve to preserve and enhance the reverence that should characterize its meetings for worship? What does the nature of the church show about the value of congregational fellowship?

2. Can an organization which has ceased to be a pillar and buttress of truth, and instead officially rejects the sound doctrine that God requires it to proclaim, be a true Christian church?

3. Since God's revelation of the mystery of godliness in verse 16 concentrates on the Person of the Lord Jesus Christ and the accomplishment of his mission, how can an adequate response to this revelation include both devotion to him and commitment to upholding those truths?

FOR STUDY 8: Read 1 Timothy 4:1–10 and chapters 12–13.

STUDY 8: 1 Timothy 4:1–10

1. Does this passage allow Christians to identify teachers marked by 'the insincerity of liars whose consciences are seared' (verse 2)? In the light of your conclusions, can you point to modern examples of men who are exposed as deceivers?

2. How is the need to train oneself for godliness vitally linked with training in the words of the faith and the rejection of irreverent and silly myths (verses 6–7)?

3. How do you assess the value of true godliness, as compared with the supposed value of ascetic practices, for your present life on earth and the prospect of heaven?

FOR STUDY 9: Read 1 Timothy 4:11–16, and chapter 14.

LET'S STUDY 1 TIMOTHY

STUDY 9: 1 Timothy 4:11–16

1. The exemplary conduct of Timothy as a Christian was to be accompanied by good practice in the life of the church, so that he would not be despised for his relative youth. What can be learnt from this in relation to all who serve the Lord?

2. How valuable to an elder is the act of ordination for the recognition and discharge of his ministry? How is it related to the gift (*charisma*) he has been given for the work?

3. How can Timothy or any elder be said to save himself and others, when Scripture makes plain that salvation is the work of God?

FOR STUDY 10: Read 1 Timothy 5:1–16 and chapters 15–16.

STUDY 10: 1 Timothy 5:1–16

1. How important is it that elders, and all Christians, regard and treat fellow Christians as members of God's family, with that love that should be exercised towards them?

2. Consider the obligations of Christians towards elderly and needy family members, especially those who are widows, in the light of scriptural principles. How are these obligations affected by various state welfare provisions?

3. Clearly the church has responsibilities for the temporal welfare of its needy members, but how is that to be worked out consistently with the teaching of 2 Thessalonians 3:10–12, especially the command, 'If anyone is not willing to work, let him not eat'?

FOR STUDY 11: Read 1 Timothy 5:17–25 and chapter 17.

STUDY 11: 1 Timothy 5:17–25

1. Should giving to provide for elders who work hard in preaching and teaching have a high priority in the church? Could it be right to withhold support from someone who is lazy?

2. Consider the importance within the church of the counsel of verses 19–21 to preserve divine standards in judging. How can we apply to ourselves and to society the principle of avoiding 'prejudging' and 'partiality'?

3. How does the guidance, 'Use a little wine for the sake of your stomach', relate to the Christian's attitude to alcoholic drinks, and to the general requirement that, since his body is sacred to the Lord, it should be preserved in good health for his use?

FOR STUDY 12: Read 1 Timothy 6:1–10 and chapters 18–19.

STUDY 12: 1 Timothy 6:1–10

1. Though forcible enslaving of men is declared to be 'contrary to sound doctrine' (1:10), there is no command here or elsewhere in the New Testament that Christian slave owners should set their slaves free. Is this inconsistent, or even a serious failure?

2. Faithful teachers of Christian doctrine who humbly submit to God's authority in the Scriptures are often accused of arrogance, yet here we are taught the opposite, namely that it is those who teach otherwise who are proud and delight in controversy. What lessons may be profitably learnt from this in assessing men's teaching?

3. How is true godliness linked with contentment?

4. Do you and other Christians really live as those convinced that 'the love of money is the root of all kinds of evil'?

FOR STUDY 13: Read 1 Timothy 6:11–21 and chapters 20–21.

STUDY 13: 1 Timothy 6:11–21

1. How significant is the descriptive phrase 'man of God' given to Timothy in relation to the charge to fulfil his ministry? In the light of 2 Timothy 3:17, does the expression apply to others?

2. Consider the impact that verses 17–19 should have on our attitude to and use of such earthly riches as have been entrusted to us by God, in the light of the very searching question in Malachi 3:8, 'Will man rob God?'

3. Fundamental elements of biblical teaching are being contradicted at this time by 'what is falsely called "knowledge"', in the realms of creation, providence and science. What should we do about these matters, if we lack the expertise of their advocates?

FOR FURTHER READING

John Calvin   *Commentary on 1 Timothy* (1556; various editions).

William Hendriksen   *New Testament Commentary: 1 & 2 Timothy and Titus*, Banner of Truth, 1960.

Geoffrey B. Wilson   *The Pastoral Epistles*, in *New Testament Commentaries*, vol. 2, Banner of Truth, 2005.

John Stott   *The Message of 1 Timothy and Titus*, *The Bible Speaks Today*, IVP, 1996.

John MacArthur   *Commentary on 1 Timothy*, Moody Press, 1995.

Simon J. Robinson   *Opening up 1 Timothy*, Day One Publications, 2004.